THE CHURCH'S AMAZING STORY

the CHURCH'S amazing story

WRITTEN AND ILLUSTRATED
BY A
TEAM OF DAUGHTERS OF ST. PAUL

Sixth Printing

ST. PAUL EDITIONS

GLORY TO GOD   PEACE TO MEN

NIHIL OBSTAT:
  THOMAS F. CASEY
  Diocesan Censor Deputatus

IMPRIMATUR:
  RICHARD CARDINAL CUSHING
  Archbishop of Boston

February 15, 1969

Library of Congress Catalog Card Number: 68—59043

Printed by the *Daughters of St. Paul*
50 St. Paul's Avenue, Jamaica Plain,
Boston, Mass. 02130

The Church's Amazing Story

There is nothing like a sense of history to give us an insight into what is going on in these times of rapid change in the Church.

THE CHURCH'S AMAZING STORY is an up-to-date, highly readable Church history. It covers every period, every struggle and triumph of that divine-human miracle that is Christ's Church.

No events, even the most controversial, are overlooked. The whole story is told honestly and vividly, with special emphasis on outstanding episodes and personalities as they move across the stage of history. And by means of end-of-chapter reflections, opportunities are offered to look at our own world and our personal lives with sharper vision and deeper insight.

One reality will strike the reader with new impact as he follows the absorbing narrative: the fact that despite internal and external trials, the Church has endured, ever young and vigorous, while all other institutions have come and gone — a fact which can only be explained by the support of that God-Man who promised her: "I will be with you all days, even to the consummation of the world."

CONTENTS

"We are the ambassadors of Christ"

St. Paul

1

THE
FIRST
BROTHE
IN
CHRIST

In the beginning,
    they called themselves "disciples,"
    because they had had a master, a founder.
Later they began to use another expression
    which seemed better suited to the
    mysterious communion which sealed their bond.
And from then on, they called themselves
    "brothers."

H. DANIEL-ROPS

The divine-human marvel that is the Church has a fascinating story behind it. The apostles of Jesus stepped out into history with a world-shattering message that was to revolutionize the lives of millions in every age to come.

The life of the first Christians was marked by tremendous faith in Jesus as the Messia expected by Israel, and by brotherly love the likes of which the world had never seen. The early Church was perfectly united under the authority of the apostles with Peter, their divinely appointed head. The Community nourished itself on the teachings of Christ and on His body and blood in the Eucharist.

From Palestine, Christianity spread throughout the Roman Empire, largely due to the efforts of the Apostle Paul.

Power out of defeat

The prophet Isaia had dramatically described the passion of the Messia and His final triumph, centuries before it happened. In his prophecy we see the Redeemer, innocent, persecuted and martyred, lifting Himself from the depths of suffering to the heights of glory and to the complete success of His redemptive mission. His victory over evil was to be stupendous. Nations and kings would gaze in amazement at the outpouring of power and glory from what seemed utter defeat and humiliation:

He was spurned and avoided by men,
a man of suffering, accustomed to infirmity,
one of those from whom men hide their faces...

Yet it was our infirmities that he bore,
our sufferings that he endured,
while we thought of him as stricken, as one
smitten by God and afflicted.
But he was pierced for our offenses,
crushed for our sins....

Because of his affliction *he shall see the light in fullness of days;*
through his suffering, *my servant shall justify many,*
and their guilt he shall bear.
Therefore I will give him his portion among the great,
and he shall divide the spoils with the mighty,
because he surrendered himself to death
and was counted among the wicked;
and he shall take away the sins of many,
and win pardon for their offenses. (Is. 53)

The disciples of Jesus

We today see the Church spread throughout the world and reaching back through the centuries, spanning great stretches of time. Its Founder had predicted this miraculous growth and permanence, despite the fact that when He left this earth on Ascension day, the band of His followers numbered only about one hundred twenty people, and none of them influential or outstanding.

If we pay close attention to what Jesus did and said, we see how carefully He planned for and organized the Church, the community of His followers. Let us try to look at the founding of our Church with new eyes, seeing it as though through the eyes of a non-Christian, a student of Christianity who is unfamiliar with the living experience that is ours. The Vatican Secretariat for Non-Christians, created after the Second Vatican Council, has written just such an account, in a brief presentation of the faith for non-Christians called "The Hope That Is in Us."

"The hope that is in us":

Jesus lived in great intimacy of prayer and dialogue with God his Father and in profound solidarity with men. He was concerned for all: men and women, the just and sinners, poor and rich, fellow citizens and strangers. His words and gestures had a liberating power for each person. If He showed any preference, it was for those who suffer, the discouraged, the humble. More than anyone before Him, He had a profound respect for each person and **He fostered in His followers a great and healthy liberty.**

Crowds came together at His arrival and accompanied Him on His journey, but He avoided a large public following and from the beginning gathered around Him only a small group of disciples and collaborators. The Gospels tell us that having prayed to His Father, He called to Himself those whom He desired, the twelve disciples, chosen to remain with Him and to go and preach His message. This is why He gave them the name of "apostles," which means "sent."

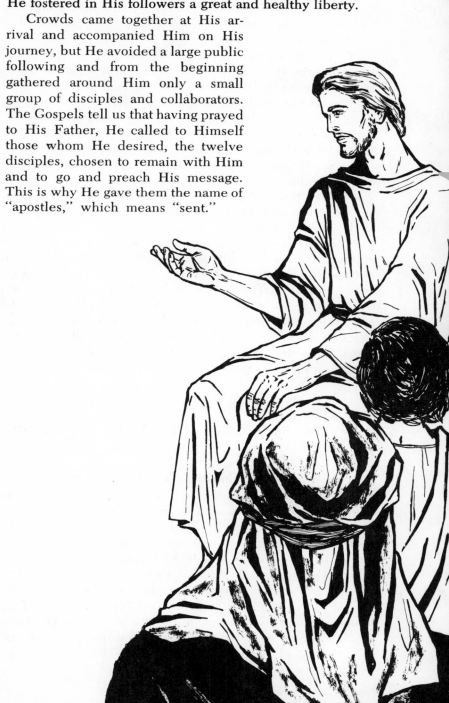

Christ gave the apostles His message, His mission, His powers. Already, while still alive, He sent them to preach in the towns and villages of Palestine. Among the apostles, He gave Peter in particular the task of leading and protecting those who would accept His message of salvation, telling him: "Strengthen your brothers...."

To Peter and the twelve Jesus promised the special assistance of the Holy Spirit so that they could faithfully transmit His message to the people. He made them responsible for the work of salvation, giving them the power to accomplish in His name acts such as Baptism, the pardon of sins and celebration of the Eucharist. This celebration was patterned after the model of the one He Himself had celebrated on the eve of His arrest and death. During the Last Supper with the twelve, He blessed the bread and the cup of wine, saying "This is my body which is to be given for you... This cup is the new covenant in my blood which is to be shed for you. Do this in memory of me."

After His resurrection, before leaving the earth, He again promised the Holy Spirit to the apostles, charging them to continue His mission: "All power has been given me in heaven and on earth; go then, making disciples of all nations, baptizing them in the name of the Father and of the Son and of the Holy Spirit, teaching them to observe all that I have commanded you. And I am with you always, even to the end of the world." As a sign of their authority, He gave them the power to perform miracles for men in the name of God.

How the apostles saw Christ in history

The apostles proclaimed Jesus Christ, the Redeemer of mankind. They knew that the coming of a Redeemer was awaited everywhere from the beginning of time. They knew this with certitude from the Bible, understood according to the teaching as they had received it from Jesus and by the light of the Holy Spirit. The first Christians, as they came in turn to the faith, felt themselves affected by an event which, inserted into human history, now dominated it completely.

The Jews recognized in Jesus Christ the fulfillment of the promises which God had made to their ancestors. The Gentiles saw themselves as the objects of an extraordinary divine benevolence which now was fully manifesting itself. The person and work of Christ, the center of a wonderful plan of Providence, was linked up with the origin of the world and coincided with the limits of history.

God, the Creator of man and of the universe, had always watched over His creatures, both individuals and nations, and had led them paternally toward the realization of their destinies in unity and in diversity.

Although rebellion and sin, and with them sickness and death, had since the beginning broken into man's history, God had always looked lovingly on His creatures, making Himself known by His works, "giving to each one life, breath and all things." The providential action of God is at the origin of nations, of civilizations, and of the religious traditions of men, to which God makes Himself known through the order of nature and of conscience, touching their hearts so that they will search for Him to "find Him if possible, by groping."

Involving themselves in the world, the apostles entered God's realm and found there traces of His presence, though they were often covered over by the egoism and the disorder of men enslaved by sin. Because of this, St. Paul calls the pre-Christian phase of salvation history "the period of God's patience and forbearance."

Not all men had lived in the same condition before Christ's coming. The apostles knew that for the sake of certain men God had in the past taken some extraordinary steps, choosing for Himself a particular people for the realization of His plan.

About 2,000 B.C., God had chosen Abraham, a just and upright Hebrew, to be the head of the People of God. With Abraham and his family God had made a covenant: He had asked Abraham to undertake freely an obedience and a moral commitment and had promised to him a blessing which would extend to the whole multitude of his descendants, and through them to all the nations of the earth. So, in His universal and providential plan, God had intervened in human history by choosing Abraham. He began with him a special dialogue: "All the nations will be blessed in your offspring."

A few centuries later, Moses gave to the descendants of Abraham a national consciousness. This was based on the experience of the extraordinary interventions of God and on the collective alliance struck by God with Abraham, making of his line "a holy nation, a priestly people"; "to proclaim the name of God to all nations." This collective alliance required obedience to the ten commandments which God had entrusted to Moses as an expression of His will. "You will have no God but me. You will not take the name of God in vain. Remember to keep holy the day of the sabbath. Honor your father and mother. Do not kill. Do not commit adultery. Do not steal. Do not bear false witness against your neighbor. Do not covet your neighbor's wife. Do not covet your neighbor's goods."

The reason for and goal of this special intervention was the formation of a people who would proclaim Him all over the earth, in view of the universal new covenant and the perfect revelation which God would bring about in the fullness of time through His ambassador, the Messia. "Messia" is a Jewish expression meaning "anointed" or "consecrated."

The giving of the New Covenant is marked by an intimate presence of God to men and by the spread all over the earth of the knowledge of God and of His love. An important text of the prophet Jeremia announces this:

"Behold, says the Lord, 'the day is coming when I will establish with Israel and with Juda a new covenant...and this is the covenant which I will establish with Israel: I will place my law in their hearts and impress it on their minds; they will be my people, and I will be their God.'" A similar text from Ezechiel adds: "I will give you a new heart, and I will place in you a new spirit,...I will place my spirit in you and you will walk in my law."

This New Covenant is the one which God established in Jesus Christ. Paul the apostle sums up this great event in these words: "In the fullness of time, God sent his Son, born of a woman, born under the law (of Moses) so that we might receive adoption as sons of God." Since that time, the covenant with the Jewish people has spread, in a new and universal kingdom, with Jesus Christ as its center: *man-God, mediator of salvation, savior of all men.*

In Him, God is present in humanity; through Him, *men are transformed and made able to approach God.*

What would you think if you read that message for the first time, perhaps after years of wondering what life is all about and whether or not God cares about you? Imagine, then, the impact of the "Good News" on those to whom it was first preached by men whose own lives had been wholly transformed through the experience of Jesus, the God-man!

No wonder that in a few years, thanks to their witness, belief in Jesus Christ spread with incredible speed!

The Church of Jerusalem

The fulfillment of Christ's command to go preach His Gospel can be said to date from Pentecost. This was a great Jewish feast, called also the Feast of Weeks and of Harvest. It occurred ten days after Christ had ascended into heaven, and His disciples had spent those days praying with Mary His Mother. On Pentecost, the Holy Spirit descended on them all, just as Christ had promised. A sound of rushing wind, the appearance of parted flames over their heads — and they were all filled with the Spirit of Jesus. The fearful, all-too-human apostles, who had seemed so ill-fit to carry on the work of the Master, were *new men*!

Now they understood many things that Jesus had told them. Now they were eager to preach Him to anyone who would listen.

On Pentecost the Jews celebrated God's revelation to Moses. Now the apostles of Jesus came forth from their hiding place in the cenacle to preach a more important revelation. Peter, who had once denied Christ out of fear,

It was a new Peter
who stepped forth to preach Christ

spoke fearlessly to crowds that had gathered, on hearing the roaring wind. Convincingly, powerfully, he proclaimed his faith in Jesus Christ. The Rock that was Peter would never again be moved by fear. Three thousand were converted that very day! The Church was on its way!

The *Acts of the Apostles* is the New Testament book that gives us the facts on the initial stages of the Christian Church, and especially on the apostolate performed by Saint Peter and Saint Paul.

In addition, we have the fourteen *Letters of St. Paul* and the seven *Catholic Letters* (one by *St. James the Less,* two by *St. Peter,* three by *St. John,* and one by *St. Jude Thaddeus*). These great books of the New Testament give us the picture of the first Christian communities. Finally there is the *Apocalypse,* or *Revelation,* of *St. John,* which encourages Christians to be strong in their faith by describing the final triumph of Jesus and His Church.

The *Acts of the Apostles* narrate that the Christian community of Jerusalem grew from day to day and won the admiration of the people for its holy, devout way of life, but especially for the brotherly love that was so evident. Although they each had their own home, they lived as one, close family. Just as Jesus and the Apostles had kept just one purse for the whole group, so the first Christians pooled all that they had and shared it with one another.

"All who believed were together and held all things in common, and would sell their possessions and goods and distribute among them all according as anyone had need. And continuing daily with one accord in the temple, and breaking bread in their houses, they took their food with gladness and simplicity of heart, praising God and being in favor with all the people" (Acts 2:44-47).

Notice the words, "with one accord," "gladness," "simplicity of heart"—what a sense of brotherhood and joyful, trusting love they evoke! This was indeed something new on the face of the earth.

"By the hands of the apostles many signs and wonders were done among the people. And with one accord they all would meet in Solomon's portico; but of the rest, no one dared to associate with them, yet the people made much of them. And the multitude of men and women who believed in the Lord increased still more, so that they carried the sick into the streets and laid them on beds and pallets that, when Peter passed, his shadow at least might fall on some of them.

And there came also multitudes from towns near Jerusalem, bringing the sick and those troubled with unclean spirits, and they were all cured" (Acts 5:12-16).

Jerusalem was filled with the preaching and wonders worked by the apostles in the name of Jesus. People watched for them as they passed. The new community made no attempt to segregate itself or to hide. Daily they met to pray together in the temple, to serve one another, to share their enthusiastic love for Christ, whose presence was so real, so vivid among them: "Where two or three are gathered together in my name, there am I in their midst," the Master had said. And how close He was!

Alarmed at the steady growth of the followers of the crucified Nazarene, the authorities ordered the apostles to keep silent. Preach no more? With that driving love burning within them? Obeying the promptings of the Holy Spirit, they fearlessly ignored the command. The salvation won by Jesus Christ must be made known!

"Go, stand and speak..."

The marvelous pentecostal period is full of events, but we can only mention the main ones:

Peter and John were arrested, sent to prison, and brought before the Sanhedrin, the Jewish high court. They were strictly charged not to speak and teach in the name of Jesus. To this the two apostles answered: "Whether it is right in the sight of God to listen to you rather than to God, decide for yourselves. For we cannot but speak of what we have seen and heard" (Acts 4: 19-20). After threatening them, the rulers and elders let them go.

Later, all the apostles were imprisoned. But during the night, an angel came to free them. He opened the doors of the prison and said to them: *Go, stand and speak in the temple to the people all the words of this life.* Exasperated, the Sanhedrin decided to put the Twelve to death. But a wise, holy Pharisee named Gamaliel saved them by telling the high priests and all the members of the Sanhedrin: "Keep away from these men and let them alone. For if this plan or work is of men, it will be overthrown; but if it is of God, you will not be able to overthrow it. Else perhaps you may find yourselves fighting even against God." So, after scourging the apostles, they freed them (cf. Acts 5:17-42).

Stephen, first of an illustrious line

St. Stephen was one of the seven deacons chosen by the apostles to be their helpers in serving the brethren and in preaching. Full of the grace and power of the Holy Spirit, he worked such great wonders among the people that some of the elders and leaders became worried and dragged him before the Sanhedrin. His face aglow, he spoke with unsurpassed ardor, and no one could withstand the wisdom of his words.

Although he clearly foresaw what would follow, Stephen reviewed for them the whole history of Israel leading up to Jesus as the Messia, and he reproved them for having opposed the Holy Spirit and murdered the Just One.

Absolutely fearless, he stood there while they gnashed their teeth in fury. Looking up to heaven, he saw the glory of God, and Jesus standing at the right hand of God. When he told them what his eyes were beholding, they rushed at him, dragged him out and stoned him to death. The dying Stephen offered his soul to God and prayed for his executioners: "Lord, do not lay this sin against them."

The persecution was on! From then on, down through the centuries, the Church of Jesus would be signed with blood, with heroes and heroines whose wills nothing could break or bend, whose dying words were of peace and forgiveness, not of hatred or revenge. Stephen was the first of a long illustrious line of martyrs unparalleled in the annals of history — witnesses to the power of the *living Christ*.

The open Church

Now, with the beginning of the persecution, the disciples fled from Jerusalem to Judea, Samaria, Phoenicia, Syria and the island of Cyprus. Everywhere they went, they spread their burning faith in Christ. Had He not said: "You will bear witness to me in Jerusalem and to the ends of the earth."

At first, only Jews were received into the Church. They were Jews of Palestine or of the *Diaspora,* which means Jews living outside Palestine in the Greek-Roman world. The apostles had addressed their message only to Hebrew communities. However, about the year 40, the Lord let Peter understand that the Church was to be open to *everyone,* including the pagans.

In a symbolic vision, Peter saw something like a sheet coming down from heaven, containing all kinds of animals. A voice said, "Arise, Peter, kill and eat!"

"Far be it from me, Lord, for never did I eat anything common or unclean." To this the voice answered, "What God has cleansed, do not call common." This strange vision taught Peter that the Mosaic Law which forbids certain foods was now abolished, and that the pagans, whom Israel had considered unclean, were also to be sanctified by the grace of Jesus Christ.

The first pagan to have the honor of entering the Church and receiving the gift of the Holy Spirit was the Roman centurion, Cornelius. Peter himself baptized him and his whole family. And the Jewish faithful were amazed that the grace of the Holy Spirit had been poured forth on the Gentiles. But God had made His will very clear, and from then on pagans flocked into the Church.

Antioch, the capital of Syria, became the center of Christians converted from paganism, just as Jerusalem was the hub of Jewish Christians. It was in Antioch that the followers of Christ were first called *Christians*.

From persecutor to apostle—
the story of Paul

A young man had stood and looked on approvingly while the elders stoned the Deacon Stephen to death. His name was Saul. He was not content for long with mere approval of persecution. Soon he became the most ferocious of persecutors.

Nothing could stop Saul the Pharisee until he was conquered and converted by Christ on the road to Damascus.

Who was this man Saul? He was a Jew of the tribe of Benjamin, born at Tarsus, a city of Cilicia, of devout Jewish parents who had become Roman citizens. Saul was his Jewish name and Paul his Roman name. As a young man, he had come to Jerusalem to study the Law of Moses under the learned holy Gamaliel. When he saw how quickly the followers of Jesus were growing in number, his fury knew no limits. To Saul, these Christians were a threat to the Mosaic Law. He thought they were corrupting the true religion by proclaiming Jesus as the Messia.

So it was that Saul persecuted them without pity. He entered "house after house, and dragging out men and women, he committed them to prison" (Acts 8:3).

But Christ was waiting for him. As he galloped toward the city of Damascus, where he knew he would find a great number of Christians, a blinding light suddenly enveloped him. Falling to the ground, he heard a voice calling him by name: "Saul, Saul, why are you persecuting me?"

"Who are you, Lord?"

"I am Jesus, whom you are persecuting. Arise, and go into the city, and there you will be told what to do...."

Now there was at Damascus a certain disciple named Ananias, and the Lord said to him in a vision, "Ananias!" And he said, "Here I am, Lord." And the Lord said to him, "Arise and go to the street called Straight and ask at the house of Judas for a man of Tarsus named Saul. He is there praying."

Paul of Tarsus — from a persecutor
of Christians to apostle of Christ

But Ananias answered, "Lord, I have heard from many about this man, how much evil he has done to your saints in Jerusalem...." The Lord said to him, "Go, for this man is a chosen vessel to me, to carry my name among nations and kings and the children of Israel. For I will show him how much he must suffer for my name" (Acts 9:10-16).

"I will show him how much he must suffer for my name," Christ had said. And Paul did not have long to wait. As soon as he began to preach about Christ, his life was threatened.

Over and over again, in the years ahead, this was to happen. But nothing would ever stop Paul.

At Antioch, he was consecrated a bishop and an apostle. Then he was sent forth by the Holy Spirit to evangelize the pagan nations.

For St. Paul, love for Christ was indelibly linked with love for the Church. Had he not heard the very voice of Christ identifying Himself with His followers: "I am Jesus *whom you are persecuting*"? Now Paul had not hunted down Jesus of Nazareth and dragged *Him* into prison.... So the only answer was that Christ and His followers were *one. To love Christ was to love the brethren.* No wonder Paul was to become a great pillar of the Church, her incomparable missionary, the teacher and doctor of true love.

From Chapter Thirteen to Chapter Twenty-eight, the *Acts of the Apostles* center around him. His field of apostolate was as unlimited as his love for Christ and men. Numberless cities heard him proclaim the good news of Christ. A band of saints and apostles followed his example. Communities grew daily in fervor and number in every city he had evangelized.

Notwithstanding beatings, chains, persecutions, dangers, shipwreck, imprisonment, hunger and sickness, spurred on by the love of Christ and the love of *truth*, Paul struggled on for thirty years, stopped by nothing, giving himself no rest. He loved Christ more than himself. This is the only explanation of the irresistible attraction felt by all who met him. This is the only explanation, too, of his fabulous success in evangelizing the countries of the northern Mediterranean, from Palestine to Rome, and probably also as far as Spain!

Around the years 40 to 42 A.D., the other apostles had begun to leave Palestine to go to the Gentiles (non-Jews), too. They divided the territory between them and spread the Faith throughout the world known at that time. Every one of them gave his life in the end as a *witness* — which is the meaning of the word "martyr" — to Jesus Christ.

The Council of Jerusalem

In the year 50 A.D., an event of considerable importance took place. By this time, the Church had already spread into Syria and parts of Asia Minor, and non-Jewish converts were growing more and more numerous. Some of the Jewish Christians began to insist that the Gentile converts should observe Jewish rites and customs.

A bitter quarrel developed over the matter, and to settle it, the apostles called a Council at Jerusalem in 50 A.D. The New Testament *Acts of the Apostles* describes it thus:

"So the apostles and the presbyters had a meeting to look into this matter. And after a long debate, Peter got up and said to them, 'Brethren, you know that in early days, God made choice among us, that through my mouth the Gentiles should hear the word of the Gospel and believe. And God, who knows the heart, bore witness by giving them the Holy Spirit just as he did to us; and he made no distinction between us and them, but cleansed their hearts by faith.

"'Why then do you now try to test God by putting on the neck of the disciples a yoke which neither our fathers nor we have been able to bear? But we believe that we are saved through the grace of the Lord Jesus, just as they are.'

"Then the whole meeting quieted down and listened while Barnabas and Paul told of the great signs and wonders that God had done among the Gentiles through them" (Acts 15:6-12).

This first General (or Ecumenical) Council is important because it clearly shows us the early Church exercising its teaching authority in matters of faith, and it also shows St. Peter exercising his authority as the Vicar of Christ and the visible head of the Church. That the others recognized his supreme position is evident from the above text: there was much disputing, but when Peter spoke, "the whole meeting quieted down."

True to the intentions of Christ her Founder, through the the decision of this first Council, the Church had decreed that converts need not observe Judaic customs; Christianity was to be *the Church for all nations.*

Especially important

▶ TO REFLECT ON:

No one felt lonely, neglected, or "outside" in the early Church because each member of the Community made it his business to "be Christ" for the others—teaching and practicing the Faith, praying for one another, sharing their possessions, comforting one another in suffering....

Are people who have strayed from God reminded of His presence by the experience of *your* Christian life?

What does an encounter with you mean for others? Can they say: "See how these Christians love one another!" as they said of Christ's first disciples?

▶ TO STRIVE FOR:

St. Paul was not imposing in appearance and he certainly got off to a bad start as far as the Christian faith went! But look what an apostle he became!

Resolve to get to know him better and try to imitate his openness to Christ. Ask him to help you do whatever Christ asks of you, so that with St. Therese of Lisieux, you can say: "I never refused the Lord anything."

▶ TO TALK TO GOD ABOUT:

In the words of St. Paul, let us pray for all our brothers, or if you wish, for someone in particular:

I bend my knees to the Father of our Lord Jesus Christ,
    from whom all fatherhood in heaven and on earth
    receives its name.
May he grant you from his glorious riches to be strength-
    ened with power through his Spirit
    to the progress of the inner man.
May Christ find a dwelling place through faith in your
    hearts.
May you be rooted and grounded in love
    so that you may be able to comprehend
    with all the saints
    which is the breadth and length and height and
    depth,
and to know Christ's love
    which surpasses knowledge.
Thus may you be filled with all the completion God has
    to give (Letter to the Ephesians, 3:14-19).

"O world! A sea of love and fight has been showered upon you! Though poor and cold, how wealthy and beautiful you are!—O Holy Church!"

Karl Adam

2

CONQUEST THROUGH SUFFERING

All who see them
shall acknowledge them as a race
the Lord has blessed.

ISAIA 61:9

As she spreads throughout the Roman Empire, the Church develops as a strongly organized body, governed by the Pope in Rome
and the bishops in communion with him. They in turn were assisted
by presbyters (priests) and deacons. Her spirit of holiness in witnessing to Christ brought converts in great numbers.

The Roman persecutions, which lasted for three centuries,
served only to strengthen faith and unity in the Church and to win
converts in unbelievable numbers. In addition it gave future ages
unparalleled examples of martyrdom faced with valor and joy. The
age of martyrs showed that the Church, like her Founder, could
turn suffering and defeat into victory.

With Constantine and Theodosius, Christianity became the religion of the Empire, and the Church could develop in peace. The
great Eastern and Western Fathers and Doctors enhanced Christian wisdom and spirituality. Despite heresies and attacks by various
groups of barbarians, the Church flourished with the guidance of
saintly, energetic popes like Gregory the Great, with the missionary
zeal of men like Patrick of Ireland, with the quest for holiness
through religious life as founded by St. Benedict.

Historians cannot explain the tremendous spread of the Christian Church by the year 600 A.D., and indeed it is impossible to say
how she won the East and the West unless we acknowledge the fact
that her Founder was ever with her as He had promised.

The glory that was Rome

Pagan Rome! Through films and novels we have been given enough of an idea of that fantastic city to feel a thrill at the sound of its name. Unrivaled in power, rich and haughty, beautiful, luxurious and incredibly cruel—such was the capital of the world to which the apostles Peter and Paul brought the Christian faith.

In our age of space travel, of electronics, of mass media, we can still appreciate the tremendous power of ancient Rome and the staggering challenge it offered the apostles. Today as tourists visit the ruins of the great estates of Rome's nobles— such as the one high on the hill beyond the Forum, overlooking the Circus Maximus, a delightful villa with its landscaped gardens, baths, decorated rooms—or as they stand in the magnificent Coliseum, they obtain some idea of the glory that was Rome and can imagine what an impression it must have made on a poor fisherman named Peter.

Yet when he and the others began to preach, Romans of both the highest and lowest classes listened...and the Community grew. Moreover, from Rome it spread into the Roman provinces like wildfire since the fine roads and efficient government made commerce and travel easy throughout the empire. And stranger still, when the mighty authorities of Rome directed the full force of persecution against the faith of Christ, they were unable to check it!

Why did so many turn from their former way of life to a completely different one? Perhaps it was the very corruption of the pagan world that made the exalted Christian ideal of purity, love and supernatural faith so attractive.

St. Paul, in his letter to the Roman Christians, does not mince words in speaking of the unbelievably corrupt moral state of pagan Rome:

"While professing to be wise, they have become fools, and they have changed the glory of the incorruptible God for an image made to corruptible man and to birds and four-footed beasts and creeping things.

"Therefore God has given them up in the lustful desires of their heart to uncleanness, so that they dishonor their own bodies among themselves—they who exchanged the truth of God for a lie, and worshiped and served the creature rather than the Creator....

"For this cause, God has given them up to shameful lusts ...to a reprobate sense, so that they do what is not fitting, being

filled with all iniquity, malice, immorality, avarice, wicked-
ness; being full of envy, murder, contention, deceit, malignity;
being...foolish, dissolute, without affection, without fidelity,
without mercy" (1:22-31).

Yes, beneath the shimmering splendor of the proud empire was the ugly reality of base idolatry, widespread hatred,
horrible cruelty to slaves, murder of the innocent, such as
handicapped children, treatment of women that degraded
them to the level of mere property for the pleasure of men,
despair and suicide, public spectacles of bloody "games" at
which the crowds acted more like wild animals than rational
men. Such was the state of the world the apostles set out to
win for Christ! (Who can say that our modern world is "impossible" to change?)

Up from darkness into joy

What tactics did the apostles use in facing such deeply
rooted and grave disorders? They proclaimed the teachings
of Jesus, His radiant examples of holiness, His love, His
grace. He had taught and practiced *poverty, purity, justice.* He
had said *to love all men as brothers.* He Himself had loved
them to the point of sacrificing His life for every one of them.

What was the result of the preaching of this good news?
It was so successful that St. Paul could write to the Roman
Christians:

"I give thanks to my God through Jesus Christ for all of
you, because your faith is proclaimed all over the world"
(Rom. 1:8).

In great numbers they moved up from the darkness and
low vice of paganism, which brought only emptiness and
misery, into the joyous light of the Gospel. The truth had made
them free! The spirit of Jesus was breathing a new, pure wind
of goodness throughout the Empire. Cruel slavery practices
began to lessen, for to the Christian, the slave was a brother in
Christ, on equal footing with the master. Eventually, slavery
disappeared entirely. Family life became holy and the home
a training ground in happy, clean living, thanks to the sacrament of Matrimony. Children were considered by Christians
as blessings from God, and women gained status, becoming
respected for their mission as wives and mothers. It was
especially the glorious example of the all-pure Virgin Mary,
whom God raised to the honor of Divine Motherhood, that

served to elevate the dignity of womankind. The thirst for power and wealth, the scorn for human life were offset by the Christian's respect for the life and property of others and his longing for the everlasting treasures of the next life.

The clash with the emperors

Since Christianity taught obedience to lawful authorities, one would not have thought that the Roman emperors would become alarmed about it. The fact is, however, that it clashed not only with the prevailing moral standards, but also with the emperor worship and the official pagan worship, which the emperors regarded as a sign of loyalty to their authority.

**Christians served as living torches
to illumine Nero's imperial gardens**

The first persecution, though, had nothing to do with these factors. It broke out in the year 64 A.D., due to a whim of the Emperor Nero. A great fire, lasting six days, had destroyed three fourths of Rome. Fearing that the fury of the populace would turn on him, Nero blamed the fire on the new Christian sect. The historian Tacitus writes that countless numbers of Christians were put to death as a result. Some were thrown to the wild animals in the arena, others crucified, others clothed in oil-soaked materials and then set ablaze, tied to poles in Nero's garden on Vatican hill, to serve as living torches!

This frightful persecution lasted from 64 to 68, the year Nero died. Unfortunately, of all the laws the insane ruler had made, the only one not repealed was the edict against the Christians.

Christianos esse non licet: "It is forbidden to be a Christian!" This law remained in force in the Roman Empire for more than *two hundred fifty years* — longer than the life span of the United States as a nation! There were, of course, periods and regions wherein the persecution was not intense. Yet, since the law was never officially repealed, any governor who was hostile to Christianity could set off a fierce local persecution. The Emperors who enforced the most violent persecutions were Nero, Domitian, Trajan, Marcus Aurelius, Septimius Severus, Decius, Valerian, and above all, Diocletian whose reign was truly the era of martyrs. Diocletian's aim was the total destruction of every thing Christian, of every single Christian.

The way they died

St. Peter and St. Paul were the most illustrious of the followers of Christ to die under Nero. St. Peter was crucified and buried on the site of the present St. Peter's Basilica. Archaeologists, in fact, have found his tomb beneath the high altar of the Basilica. St. Paul, a Roman citizen, was given the Roman death of decapitation outside the city. One can still visit the dark underground cell where he spent his last night on earth. In this cell, as in the Mamertine prison where he was held with St. Peter, the words of Paul to the Romans come to mind:

"Who will separate us from the love of Christ? Shall tribulation, or distress, or persecution...or the sword?...We overcome because of him who has loved us" (8:35, 37).

Under Domitian, the apostle St. John was sent to Rome to undergo a martyr's death in a cauldron of boiling oil, but God miraculously preserved him. He was later exiled to the island of Patmos. Under Trajan and the "Antoninian" Emperors, famous martyrs were Pope St. Clement, a disciple of St. Peter; St. Simon, Bishop of Jerusalem; and St. Ignatius, Bishop of Antioch, who declared he was anxious to be ground by the teeth of the beasts so as to be pure wheat for Christ!

When the elderly Bishop of Smyrna, St. Polycarp, a disciple of St. John the Evangelist, was urged by the proconsul to

**St. Blandina — she comforted
and encouraged her fellow martyrs**

blaspheme Christ so as to save himself, he replied, "For eighty-six years I have served Him and He has shown me nothing but goodness; how could I insult Him now?" With that he walked to his execution with the majesty of a patriarch.

A thing called courage

In Lyons (modern-day France), under Marcus Aurelius, a bitter persecution broke out which was described in detail by the Christian community there in a letter to the Church at Vienne. The account of the heroism of a frail slave girl named Blandina is especially moving. Tortured in every way possible, she refused to yield: "I am a Christian! And we don't do anything wrong!" Every attempt to sway this seemingly delicate creature was like ramming against an iron wall. She it was who sustained the courage of the others as they faced death and then she herself expired.

Of every age, from the ninety-year-old Bishop Photinus to the twelve-year-old St. Vitus; of every social class; of every position in the Church, from Pope to bishops, to deacons, to lay men and women; of every part of the Empire, from Africa to Palestine to Europe—these were the martyrs, numbering in the millions, whose blood was the seed of future Christians.

Throughout the whole period, the Church grew stronger in faith and love, in unity, in its understanding of Christ and His message. Christians gathered together, often in underground catacombs, to hear the word of God as recorded by the evangelists such as Luke, who had been St. Paul's companion, and Mark, who had recorded St. Peter's preaching. Fervently they would celebrate the Eucharist and receive Holy Communion, the Bread of the Strong. Christ was very much in their midst as they gathered about the Holy Father in Rome, or their bishop in other cities, to pray for one another and to pray for those who were persecuting them.

**Constantine at Milvian Bridge—
the victory was Christ's**

Constantine

The entrance on the scene of the complex and fascinating Emperor Constantine brought the persecutions to an end. Though he himself was baptized only on his deathbed, and though he was to be guilty of murdering his wife and son, his reign brought recognition of Christianity as a lawful religion. His own mother, the Empress St. Helena, did much to make the faith of Christ esteemed in the Empire. It is said that the reason Constantine looked with such favor on Christianity was that just before the battle of Milvian Bridge, 313 A.D., in which he defeated his rival for the throne, he had seen a cross shining in the sky in broad daylight, together with the words, "By this sign you will conquer!" On the following night, Christ appeared to him and invited him to have a standard made in the form of a cross. From then on, the armies of Constantine bore this triumphant standard. Now the Church could emerge from the catacombs!

Great Christian churches were built by Constantine and his saintly mother. The Church began to organize better now that she could breathe the air of freedom. Councils of bishops were held in various cities, and the faithful were organized into formal dioceses and metropolitans, or archdioceses, in the larger cities. In this way, it was easier for the ministers of Christ to tend to the needs of their people.

Heresies

In the fourth, fifth and sixth centuries, the Church had two major struggles to face: heresies and the invading barbarians.

At the very time when outward persecution was ending, she was confronted with the far greater danger of internal division, of schism, of error which was winning members from the true faith. Many Christians did not recognize the error being taught by the heretics, who often used the same, familiar words of Catholic teaching while meaning something quite different.

There were various types of heresies and schismatic groups. Even in previous centuries, there had been men like Montanus and Marcion who had taught error. But the Church had been rather small at the time. Now, instead, the Church was large; it is estimated that by the beginning of the fourth century, there may have been as many as six to ten million Christians in the Roman Empire alone. Heretics such as Arius actually formed whole counter-churches by leading astray great numbers from communion with the mother Church. Such deviations from the teachings of the Church aroused true believers to fever pitch, so ardent was their faith, and many went to their death rather than yield on any point of faith or on allegiance to the authority of the Pope of Rome and the bishops, the successors of Peter and the apostles.

Why did heresies develop? There are a number of reasons, some as ordinary as pride. A man who had proclaimed a new doctrine and had gained a following might not have the honesty to renounce his error when the Church's authorities reproved it. At other times, men converted to Christianity brought some of their former pagan notions with them, or certain false philosophical ideas, which they tried to blend into the Christian teaching.

Major heresies centered, as we would expect, on the crucial question of Jesus Himself. There were those who said that Jesus Christ was indeed God, but not truly human, not a real man. On the opposite side were those who said that Jesus Christ was a great man, through whom God did great things for mankind, but they denied that Christ was God.

The Arian heresy, the most powerful the Church ever had to face, held the last-named position: that Christ was not God in essence, but rather an exceptional creature who achieved perfection by His own will alone. So clever was Arius in spreading his doctrine, in hiding his errors under pious language, that the heresy spread far and wide, despite the united efforts of the Church and Constantine to stop it. Constantine passionately desired to preserve the truth and the unity of Christendom, yet he himself became confused and at times was won over by the heretics. Moreover, the interference by an emperor in a theological, doctrinal dispute, no matter how good his intentions, was to set a pattern for more such interference, which would be a great danger for the Church in the future.

The great Church Fathers and Doctors

The Arian heresy met its match in the marvelous defenders of the true faith who appeared on the scene. The greatest of these was Athanasius, a man who dominates the whole turbulent period, who defied the heretics, outwitted their every attempt to trap him, and preached the divinity of Christ with a passion and relentless energy that neither five painful exiles and the constant threat of death could stop. Moreover, Athanasius resisted the intervention of the emperor, Constantine's son, in the affairs of the Church, and he governed his diocese while in hiding when hunted by the imperial police. Nothing could stop this champion of the Church! He was the first non-martyr bishop raised to the honors of sainthood.

Arianism, like the other heresies, lived on after the sudden and horrible death of its founder, Arius, but by the end of the fourth century, it had just about spent itself, and the true doctrine of the divinity of Christ, defined by the General Council of Nicea, was recognized everywhere.

This is a good point at which to speak of the Fathers and Doctors of the Church, outstanding personalities who have left their mark not only on Church history, but on the history of education, psychology, political theory, philosophy, and culture in general. Besides St. Athanasius we can name Saints *Augustine, Jerome, Ambrose, John Chrysostom, Gregory of Nazianzus, Gregory of Nyssa....* By their writings and their sermons which people flocked to hear, these great lights of learning and virtue opened the minds of men to the treasures of the Bible. They nourished Christian devotion, courageously spoke out against those layfolk and clerics who were living scandalous lives. By their own example of love for all, of deep faith, of fervor in prayer, particularly in their worship of Christ in the Eucharist, these saints showed their own era and centuries to come what it means to live the Christian ideal to the fullest. In their unforgettable works, we find the Catholic Faith as we know it today, in its doctrines, in its commandments and morals, in its sacraments, its liturgy leading us to *live Christ*, in its devotions to the saints, and among these, to Mary, the Mother of God, in particular.

Augustine

St. Augustine is perhaps the most interesting of them all, and the best known, even by many non-believers in our day who know him only as the writer of the amazingly honest *Confessions*. This classic, one of the world's most popular books, is the story of his life, especially of his conversion. It is recognized as a great autobiography, the beginning of a real study of the human personality (psychology). In it, the famous bishop of the North African city of Hippo tells of his boyhood, of his teen years, of his sins, of his attraction to the wierd Manichaean religion, of his struggle to give up sinful pleasures in order to embrace Christianity.

With complete frankness, Augustine recounts what he went through, the struggle he experienced between the attraction of Christ and the pull of his flesh. In reading the *Confessions*, millions of people have felt as though they were reading their *own* story.

The young Augustine

Once converted, Augustine went all the way. He became a priest, and later, despite his reluctance, a bishop. He who had once scorned the Sacred Scriptures because they did not have the polished style he loved and admired in Latin writers such as Cicero, now nourished his soul on them and shared his love for the word of God with us all. The great mysteries of life, of time, of the human mind and memory; the mysteries of faith such as the Blessed Trinity, the Incarnation; the drama of the Church in the world and in history—all these topics were given an unsurpassed treatment by this genius. His works became the basis of Christian studies in theology, philosophy, history and Scripture.

Never satisfied with what he had done, always eager to win more people to Christ, Augustine worked right up to his death, which occurred as the barbarian Vandals were attacking the city.

Barbarian invaders

Trials and sufferings awaited the Church in the form of the barbarian invasions. Who were the barbarians? They were numerous tribes from the North and the East who had long been eyeing the civilization and the wealth of the Empire with envy. As long as Rome maintained its power, they could do little except attack the outlying frontiers here and there, which they did during the second and third centuries. But when the Romans became soft and dissolute, and the Empire was torn by rival parties, full scale invasions began.

The fourth century saw hordes of savage tribes pouring in, killing, burning and pillaging everywhere: Visigoths, Huns, Vandals, Ostrogoths, Lombards, Burgundians, Franks. ...Wave after wave, they came in seemingly endless attacks, in Germany, Gaul (modern France), Italy, Roman Africa and Spain. They took over cities and set themselves up in complete power, copying the Roman system of rule, which they greatly admired.

It seemed to many that the fall of Rome in the year 410 marked the end of all civilization. Throughout the former Empire, the various groups of barbarians were in complete control. Christianity seemed to have been dealt a death blow, too. But such was not to be. Strong with the power of God, the Church checked the ferocity of the conquerors, won them by her moral strength, softened their savagery, and converted them to her Gospel, to the Christian way of life.

We can assert that the Church was saved and the barbarians were converted and civilized mainly by the efforts of the bishops and the monks.

When the marauders swept down upon the European cities, the people were, for the most part, left defenseless. The imperial government and its soldiers were powerless to deal with the situation. The only champions of the people were the bishops, and at this period, the Church was blessed with bishops of tremendous character. Time and again, they were defenders of their cities, as were the Popes of Rome. And very often, risking their lives, they went through enemy lines to confront the barbarian chiefs personally, seeking the best terms possible, trying to dissuade them from burning and looting.

Such men were St. Germanus of Auxerre, St. Exsuperius of Toulouse, St. Quovultdeus of Carthage, St. Nicasius of Rheims, St. Lupus of Troyes, St. Anianus of Orleans, and many

Rome's terror—the
barbarian invasions

more. These were men of first rank, strongly self-disciplined, humble of heart, fearless and confident in God, wise and totally dedicated to their people.

No wonder the savage invaders felt admiration for their Roman fortitude, their intelligence, leadership and obvious holiness!

Light spreads out from Rome

It is marvelous to note how the barbarian kings were awed and fascinated by Christian Rome. In 410, when Alaric sacked Rome, he ordered that the basilicas of the apostles built by Constantine were to be left untouched. Thus, the terrified people flocked to them as safe places of refuge. And in 452, when Attila, called the Scourge of God, was leading his Huns toward Rome, destroying everything in their path, he was met by the great Pope, Leo I, who faced him without fear and ordered him in the name of God to respect the holy city. Behind the majestic figure of the Pontiff, Attila seemed to behold the apostles Peter and Paul warning him, and he at once sounded a retreat.

The people of Italy and Rome, who had been left unprotected in that period of terror, gathered around the Vicar of Christ as their only hope of safety. And the Pope protected the oppressed, evangelized the victors, gathered up from the ruins all that was good in the Roman heritage: language, customs and laws.

Just as ancient Rome had sent her consuls and proconsuls to rule over other peoples, so *Christian Rome* began to send her bishops and missionaries to bring the light of the Gospel and civilization to the barbarous nations.

Once converted, these nations became the most ardent defenders of the Church and the Christian faith.

In the sixth century, the peoples who had conquered Spain were converted. In the same period, Clovis and his valiant Franks received Baptism. Clovis had been won to Christianity by the example of his wife, the Burgundian princess, St. Clotilda. In Italy, the devout Queen Theodolinda was instrumental in obtaining the conversion of the Lombards.

St. Patrick in Ireland, St. Augustine of Canterbury in England, St. Boniface in Germany, Saints Cyril and Methodius among the Slavs, St. Avitus among the Burgundians, St. Martin of Braga among the Suevians — and thus, in the end, Europe was won to the Church of Christ.

The men of Benedict

When the invasions had reduced Europe to a vast wasteland of destroyed cities and burnt fields, it was principally the monks of St. Benedict who built it up again. Benedict of Nursia had left the world to live as a hermit, in imitation of the many men in both the East and the West who freely chose a life of solitude, prayer and penance, to achieve union with Christ and to obtain blessings for the world. But Benedict's mission was to be the founding of communities of holy men who would live together under a rule, pray together and work together. At Montecassino, near Rome, he founded the most famous monastery in the West, from which monks left to start similar monasteries throughout Europe.

Ora et labora, "Work and pray," was the Benedictine rule of life. Tirelessly, the monks labored to turn deserted fields into flourishing vineyards, orchards and farmlands. They cleared forests, drained swamps, built roads and bridges. Around their numerous abbeys, towns grew up and trade again began to prosper. People took new hope at the sight of what could be accomplished by faith, prayer and hard but satisfying and creative labor. Those magnificent monasteries were oases of learning and holiness. In them, the sacred sciences were taught, as well as the basic studies and also practical arts, such as carpentry and farming. It was in these religious houses that the famous work of copying precious manuscripts by hand went on—the Bible, the works of the great Fathers of the Church, and also the famous Roman and Greek writers and philosophers. Without the monks, these classics would have been lost to the world.

The poor were always welcome, fed and sheltered at the monasteries; travelers could find rest and meals there; the infirmaries of the abbey were the forerunners of public hospitals. In every way, the monasteries could be called the schools, hospitals and social welfare agencies of the time.

Just as the martyrs had witnessed to Christ through their deaths for the Faith, so the monks witnessed to Him through their lives of prayer and generous charity towards all.

Gregory

The last Pope of this period, just before the Middle Ages, was St. Gregory the Great. The first monk to become a Pope, he greatly encouraged the Benedictines in their work. Pope Gregory reformed many practices in the music and liturgy of the Church, wrote directives for Catholic priests to follow, books explaining the Gospels, and lives of many saints. He drew the Christian peoples into closer unity, and so great was his good influence that throughout the Christian world, men looked with confidence for help and guidance to the papacy.

It was Pope Gregory who worked so hard for the conversion of the various pagan or Arian groups. He sent St. Augustine of Canterbury and his band of monks to the Angles and Saxons in England, and other missionaries to the Lombards. He supported St. Leander in his apostolate to the Visigoths in Spain.

The work of converting and civilizing was a gigantic task, but the popes, the bishops and the monks persevered, and they succeeded.

Especially important

▶ TO REFLECT ON:

Not all Christians were martyrs. Some, when faced with the prospect of inhuman torture, imprisonment in horrible dungeons, condemnation to a living death in mines, or the capital punishment in the bloody arena—some apostasized out of fear. They were few in proportion to the millions who found strength in Christ, strength beyond their natural power.

When St. Felicitas became a mother in prison, the birth pains caused her to wail and cry. One of the jailors tauntingly asked her how she would act when she had to face the wild beasts if she was crying so in childbirth. To this, the slave girl calmly replied: "When I am in the amphitheater, Someone else will be within me, and He will suffer for me, and I in Him."

With what trust in Christ do we face the sacrifices and challenges of being a true Christian in every situation that comes up, in temptations we face, whether alone or with others?...

▶ TO STRIVE FOR:

You as a Christian have to be a witness of Jesus in the specific vocation He gives you. Make every effort now to grow in strength, in self-control, in prayerful union with Him, especially through Holy Communion, so that you will be ready for the work in life He has prepared for you.

At times you feel sure of yourself and unafraid; other days you feel almost helpless and overwhelmed with doubts. This is a painful situation, but make the most of it. When you feel good and confident, ask the Divine Master to give you His strength, which is the only lasting kind. When you feel hesitant and weak, put all your trust in Him and act *as though* you were courageous. The courage will come, even to your own surprise!

▶ TO TALK TO GOD ABOUT:

Pray with modern-day sufferers, with the Lithuanian Catholic girls, now in a Siberian concentration camp, whose little hand-written book of prayers was smuggled out to the free world:

O Lord God, forgive my sins
 and give me the strength to do what I have to do.
 May I do it all perfectly!
To Your greatest sacrifice,
 to the merits of all Your saints
 gathered in the treasury of the Church,
 join my sufferings:
  the weariness,
  the scorn,
  the tears of homesickness,
  the hunger and cold,
  all the ills of soul,
  my efforts...
 for a better future
  for all those I love.
Lord, have mercy
 on those who persecute and torture us!
Give to them, too,
 the grace
 to know the sweetness of Your love.
          Amen.

O Lord, let your abiding mercy purify and defend the Church. Graciously govern her always, for without Your assistance, she cannot remain safe.

FIFTEENTH SUNDAY AFTER PENTECOST

"God wills it!"
Rallying Cry of the Crusaders

3

LIGHT
AND
DARKNESS

Even in her darkest hours,
The Church will never die:

"You are built upon the foundation
      of the apostles and prophets
with Christ Jesus himself
as the chief cornerstone."

EPHESIANS 2:20

Being both human and divine, the Church presents "light and shadows" as we follow her exciting course through history. In the period when evil men crippled her from within her own ranks, the darkness seemed to envelop her. But she came out of this darkest of hours essentially unharmed and moved on to new spiritual conquests.

This chapter, then, gives the history of the growth of the Church's tremendous influence, her acquisition of lands, the accomplishments of Charlemagne, the Moslem threat, the evils within the Church and the reform movement, the crusades, and the Greek schism.

The Church's story, like history itself, throbs with life, color, action.

The patrimony of Peter

The Gospel seed had been sown. The empire had tried to crush it, but the Church had grown even more, and developed its doctrines, organization, and worship, blessed by the holiness and wisdom of its Fathers and Doctors. Finally, it had become the one great spiritual power in the western world, conscious of its responsibility not only for men's souls, but also for their life in this world.

The imperial government in Constantinople, the city which Constantine had made his capital, had washed its hands of the defense of Italy against the barbarian invaders. Even the emperor's officials had fled their court at Ravenna when the invaders approached. The Popes thus had been obliged to negotiate with the leaders of hostile armies and to organize the military defense of Rome or other cities. Circumstances compelled them to be the protectors of the people. They were, therefore, endowed with temporal as well as spiritual power.

Another reason for the temporal power of the Vicars of Christ is what is called the *Patrimony of St. Peter.* This word applies to the tremendous gifts of estates, farms, and even towns which devout, noble families had made to the Popes, so that the Church could have means to help the needy and spread the faith. These property gifts were to be found all over the western empire, but most of them were located in Italy.

Finally, in the middle of the eighth century, another circumstance made the Popes the rulers of a large part of central Italy. The fierce Lombards were attacking Rome, and Pope Stephen III was forced to turn to the Frankish king, Pepin the Short, for help. He had appealed to the invaders for mercy, he had begged for help from the emperor in the East, and both efforts had failed. The emperor did not even bother to reply to the Pope.

King Pepin with his armies twice crossed over into Italy and forced the Lombards to surrender the lands they had captured. But to whom were these cities to be handed over? The people of the region by now despised the imperial power at Constantinople because the emperors there followed the Iconoclast heresy. Since this heresy fanatically rejected all veneration of images, the emperor's men had ruthlessly destroyed sacred shrines and statues. Moreover, the eastern rulers had destroyed many of the farmlands belonging to the

Patrimony of St. Peter. Finally, they had abandoned Italy when the Lombards were attacking. The people's loyalty was wholly with the Pope of Rome, whom they felt to be their true leader and protector. So King Pepin donated to the Holy See the towns and territories he had won, as a free and independent possession. This land became known as the Papal States. It kept the Holy Father independent and gave him the possibility of doing much good, even on the natural level. However, it brought problems, too, just as the intervention by Pepin was both a blessing and the beginning of new problems.

Charlemagne

Pepin's successor to the Frankish throne was one of the most illustrious rulers the world has ever known. He was called Charles the Great, "Carolus Magnus" in Latin, and is known in history as Charlemagne. He had his personal faults, among them ruthlessness and cruelty—he even forced his pagan enemies, the Saxons, to be converted at sword-point! But he was a stupendous statesman, soldier, law-giver, promoter of education and staunch defender of Christianity.

Charlemagne and his mighty empire

Marching rapidly through swamps and forests, fighting bloody battles on one campaign after another, Charlemagne destroyed the power of the Lombards and left the Papacy completely free at last. He invaded the Moslems in Spain; he conquered the pagan Avars and Saxons. Throughout his vast kingdom, he continually promulgated laws to support the Christian religion in every way. He did all he could to see to it that priests were well educated and worthy of their office.

On Christmas Day, in the year 800, in St. Peter's in Rome, Pope St. Leo III crowned Charlemagne Emperor of the West and the *Holy Roman Empire* came into being. Charlemagne already owned practically everything in Western Europe, so this coronation brought him no new possessions, but it did result in a new Christian Empire, wherein emperor and Pope would work together for the temporal and spiritual good of the Christian people.

Though his intentions were the best, Charlemagne began a practice that was to be a bitter thorn in the side of the Church. He would interfere in purely religious matters, such as the choice of new bishops or the regulation of worship. His

**Mohammed —
from an ancient Moslem document**

successors were to follow his example and cause great harm. No wonder some nicknamed him the "Christian Caliph," after the fighting religious leaders of Mohammedanism.

Mohammed and the Moslems

No one could have suspected that the greatest threat to Christendom would come from the barren, unknown land of Arabia, whose small population of nomads was always fighting among themselves. The man who united them under his religious leadership was Mohammed, who was born in the latter half of the sixth century. At first tormented by religious problems and doubts, he came forth at last with a new religion, called *Islam*, drawn somewhat from Christianity and Judaism. His creed was simple: *"There is no God but Allah (the one true God), and Mohammed is his prophet."* The word "Islam" itself means: "Absolute submission to God's will."

Followers of Islam were forbidden to adore other gods, to commit adultery, to change to another religion, to gamble, to eat pork, or to drink wine. They had to follow certain prayer rituals, fast and go on pilgrimage. All were obliged to propagate the faith.

Though Islam developed as a warring religion bent on conquest, and though many practices differed greatly from Christianity—a man could lawfully have four wives, for example—still there were and there are many truths held in common by Moslems and Christians. Islam demands worship of God alone, who is adored as all-powerful and eternal; it professes belief in the existence of angels; it holds the Scriptures as sacred (together with the Koran, the book of the writings of Mohammed); it professes belief in prophets and apostles, including Jesus (who, however, is not held to be God); it looks forward to the day of judgment and resurrection, and it believes in heaven and hell.

Stopped by "the Hammer"

Mohammedan conquests in a very short while were fantastic. By the early part of the eighth century, they were in

Charles Martel and his
Franks stopped the
Moslems at Tours.

control of the greater part of the lands around the Mediterranean Sea. Spain was completely won and they were beseiging Constantinople. It seemed as though Europe and the whole of Christendom, in the East and the West, would fall, just as Syria, Palestine, Egypt, Northern Africa and Spain had fallen. The tide of Mohammedan conquest seemed about to wipe out the religion of Christ. But the tide turned.

In the East, the Moslems were defeated at Constantinople, and in the West, Charles Martel and his Franks stopped them at Tours in 732. That battle between Charles "the Hammer" and the Moslem Abd-er-Rahman was one of the most dramatic in history because of all that depended on it and because of the complete contrast between the two armies. The two civilizations showed in the very way they dressed and fought: The Arabians in white, flowing clothes charged down on the enemy; the Franks in heavy mail and iron helmets standing their ground like a sturdy wall. The wall never broke, and the Arabs were defeated.

The Dark Ages

The term, "Dark Ages," is sometimes mistakenly applied to the whole medieval period, but the fact is that it fits only the century and a half following the death of Charlemagne. The Empire was divided up between his grandsons and then into many little, semi-independent territories all fighting each other. To make matters worse, more savage invasions afflicted all Europe. Besides the Moslems known as the Saracens, who once attacked Rome and sacked the Basilicas of Saints Peter and Paul, and who constantly raided many parts of Italy, there were the pagan Magyars pouring over the eastern frontier. They roamed all over Europe, burning and killing, until they were stopped in 955. They settled in Hungary and through the work of a great king, St. Stephen, they were eventually converted to Christianity.

The Danes and the Vikings were the worst scourge of all. They were expert sailors and would land at little-used spots, attack and loot a town, and then be off before any counterattack could be made. Later on, they began to conquer and set up kingdoms, as in Ireland, France and England. Eventually, the Christian rulers were able to defeat these Norsemen, but the devastation and terror of the century and a half of invasions left its marks on the affairs of the Church.

In all the turmoil, bishops, abbots and priests often had to appeal to local lords for protection, and many unscrupulous tyrants would then demand in return a right to put "their own man" into Church positions. Some of the powerful families thus succeeded in having unworthy members made bishops, and the Church has never known such evil bishops as there were in these cases. They broke their vow of celibacy openly, fought battles, were brutal and dishonest. Moreover, they appointed unworthy, ignorant men as priests who lived as sinfully as the bishops.

Scandals in high places

Not even the papacy was spared. Bloody rivalry went on between Roman aristocrats to put their members on the throne of Peter so as to rule the Papal States. As a result, some shameful scandals came from the highest office in the Church! . Though the majority were not evil, there were at least two unworthy Popes at this time, and it was indeed a dark hour for Christ's Church.

Yet the remarkable fact is that none of these Popes ever proclaimed false doctrines on faith or morals. Their personal lives and motives may have been disgraceful, but the Church came through this crisis — as through all others — unharmed. Moreover, from time to time, zealous reforming Pontiffs acceded to the Papacy, the greatest of these being St. Nicholas I, who fearlessly resisted and denounced the evils of his day.

The real upward swing of reform began about the middle of the eleventh century. Its chief mover was Cardinal Hildebrand, who later became Pope St. Gregory VII, but other important figures involved were Pope St. Leo IX, Pope Nicholas II, who decreed that Popes should be elected by cardinals and not chosen by political leaders, St. Peter Damian, and the Countess Matilda of Tuscany, who used her wealth and troops to protect the Pope against opponents of reform.

The religious congregation of Cluny also played a major role in promoting new fervor and reform among monks and in ridding the Church of the scandal of unworthy abbots. At Cluny, a fervent monastery had been founded which rejected all the sins of the age, and over which saintly abbots presided. Subject to the Pope's authority alone, it was free of interference from evil men, lay or clerical. From this motherhouse, over three hundred other monasteries were founded, all observant of the strict Benedictine way of life, all edifying and building up the Church. The ten thousand Cluny monks were a great factor in the reform.

From Cluny a light went forth

A fearless Pope and a ruthless king

But it was the valiant Pope St. Gregory VII who fought and suffered the most. He deposed all bishops who had paid to get into office (the sin called simony) or who were living impurely. He appealed to the loyal Christian people to avoid unworthy shepherds, and he excommunicated any priest, bishop or abbot who received a bishopric or abbey from a lay person. He also decreed that any king would be excommunicated if he invested anyone with the symbols of bishops or abbots. This was the evil known as "lay investiture."

"Selling" bishoprics and abbeys had been a favorite game with Emperor Henry IV of Germany. When he scornfully disobeyed the decree, the Pope was forced to excommunicate him and absolve all his subjects from their obligation to obey him. It was the only way to stop the horrible evils and scandals and leave the Church free to choose worthy men as bishops.

Frightened, Henry dressed as a penitent and went to Canossa, where the Pope was staying at the time, to beg forgiveness. For three days he stood in the snow outside the Countess Matilda's castle in Canossa, begging the Pope to absolve him. St. Gregory did, but he had his doubts about Henry's sincerity.

Soon enough, Henry was back in Italy, this time to attack the Vicar of Christ. He captured Rome, but Pope Gregory held out in the Castel Sant'Angelo, a fort dating back to ancient Roman times, and still standing today. When he summoned troops of Normans from Sicily to his aid, Henry fled. Still the saintly Pope ended his days in exile, suffering to the very end. His reform, however, was a success, and never again would the Church be so chained down by secular interference.

**Pope St. Gregory VII
and an insincere royal penitent**

The crusaders

"Crusader"—the word has come down in history with a thrill and a glory all its own. Why? Perhaps because of the sheer beauty of ideals that inspired the unique, almost unbelievable movement called the crusades. Men "took the cross" for Christ, to recapture the land made holy by the Son of God while He lived on earth. For hundreds of years it had been in the possession of the Mohammedans. Moreover, the Moslem leadership had passed from the Arabs to the ferocious Fatimites of Egypt and, in the second half of the eleventh century, to the Seljuk Turks. Thus, the Christians of Palestine and Syria were ruthlessly persecuted. Western pilgrims to the Holy Land were also subjected to the same treatment.

When the Turks conquered Asia Minor and stood at the gates of Constantinople, it again looked as though the Eastern Empire was doomed. Pope St. Gregory had hoped to send an army under Emperor Henry IV to aid the Christians there, but his struggle with Henry over reform made it impossible. It was his successor, Pope Urban II, who started the First Crusade in 1095.

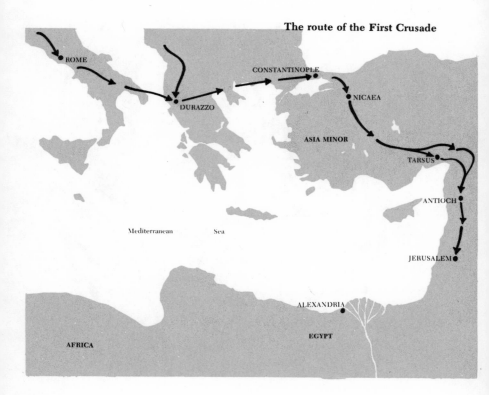

The route of the First Crusade

The period of the crusades spans about two hundred years, from 1095 to 1291. There were about seven major crusades and several minor expeditions. The Popes were always the inspirers and organizers, and they kept alive the religious ideals of the crusaders.

Pope Urban himself was amazed at the overwhelming response to his first appeal for armies to help the Christian brethren of the East and to free the Holy Sepulcher. *"God wills it!"* was the enthusiastic cry that time after time interrupted his talk. *Three hundred thousand* men vowed to go to Jerusalem to fight for the cause of Christ!

Some of the crusades were successful, some were disastrous failures. A Latin kingdom was set up in Palestine where Christians could live and freely worship at the holy shrines of Christianity. It lasted about a century. Military orders of warrior-monks fought bravely to defend it when the Turks re-attacked it, as was inevitable. Eventually however, being far outnumbered, they lost the kingdom and Jerusalem to Saladin, the best of Moslem fighters. One of the greatest of the crusader-kings, Richard the Lion-Hearted, of England displayed tremendous heroism in the Third Crusade and won back several cities, obtaining permission for free pilgrimages to the Holy Sepulcher.

The Fourth Crusade was a disgrace inasmuch as it ended with a serious armed conflict between Eastern and Western Christians, and the capture of Constantinople by part of the crusading army, which should have been on its way to Jerusalem! The Sixth and Seventh Crusades were led by the valiant St. Louis, King of France, whose behavior in captivity made such an impression on the Saracens that they offered to make him their king! Freed, St. Louis undertook another expedition but was struck down by disease in Tunis.

A fantastic gesture of faith

At the end of the crusading era, the Holy Land was still in Moslem hands, but the crusades had saved Europe from infidel invasion. Spain, too, in a decisive battle, was forever freed of the Moslem threat. Moreover, the crusades had united Western Christendom and stopped its princes from fighting among themselves. Much new knowledge — geographical, scientific and navigational — was gained. New trade relations were established. Religious fervor, above all, increased.

It would be ridiculous to look upon every crusader as a saint or even as a deeply religious man. Indeed, a number of the leaders, such as Frederick II, were greedy, ambitious men. There was, in short, a very human side to the saga of the crusades. But despite this, the only explanation for such a fantastic gesture on the part of hundreds of thousands—who left home and country to risk their lives for the sake of their brethren in the faith and to free sacred shrines—is their deep love of Jesus Christ.

Typical of these truly devout, heroic men was Godfrey de Bouillon, Duke of Lorraine, who led the first crusade, in which Jerusalem was captured and the Christian kingdom established. He humbly refused to accept the title of king, and so was proclaimed "Defender of the Holy Sepulcher." When offered a crown of gold, he would not wear it, declaring that it was not right for him to wear a golden crown in the spot where "the King of kings had worn a crown of thorns."

Crusaders, soldiers of the cross

**Louis of France,
a saint on the throne**

"The crusaders battled so bravely because they believed that they were fighting for the cause of Christ. They placed the cross on their shoulders that they might offer Christ cross for cross, suffering for suffering, that they might by mortifying their desires share with Christ in the resurrection. So motivated, the soldier of the cross looked upon failure and death as no less blessed than success and victory. Such idealism made the crusades one of the most inspiring enterprises in all history" (Martin Harney, S.J., *The Catholic Church through the Ages*).

The East-West split

A deep wound in the unity of Christendom was the break between the greater part of the Church in the East and the

Church in the West. Today, that wound is still open, but there are hopeful signs of growth toward its healing.

The actual and final break came in 1054, when the Patriarch of Constantinople, Michael Cerularius, rejected the primacy of the Pope and led the great majority of Eastern Christians out of communion with the Vicar of Christ and the rest of the Church. But this one bishop could not have brought about such a disaster unless the crisis had been gradually building up for a long time.

We can trace the trouble to a number of causes, principally the ambition of Emperors at Constantinople to rule the Church, for which reason they tried to make the Bishop of Constantinople equal to or greater than the Pope; the ill-will caused by the Iconoclast heresy, which had the support of the imperial power; the lack of communication between the East and West due to Moslem control of the Mediterranean sea route; and especially the lack of understanding due to differences in culture, language, practices and political views. The Eastern peoples had been especially displeased at the establishment of the new Roman Empire in the West when the Pope crowned Charlemagne.

Before the final break, there were several other schisms, the most famous being the one involving the great scholar Photius, which occurred in 857. The Patriarch of Constantinople, St. Ignatius, resigned, forced by Bardas, the evil uncle of Emperor Michael III. Photius was elected by a council of bishops to take his place. Some Easterners were displeased and appealed to Pope St. Nicholas I, who upheld St. Ignatius. The schism that resulted lasted ten years; at the death of St. Ignatius, Rome recognized Photius as Patriarch, and the schism ended. But the ill feelings that had been aroused persisted.

In 1043, when Michael Cerularius became Patriarch, he attacked the practices of the Church in the West in a violent manner and closed all Latin-rite churches in Constantinople. He was determined to bring about a schism and even erased the Pope's name from the liturgy. At that the Holy Father's legates (personal representatives) excommunicated him, and the schism became a reality.

Thus, although there were some doctrinal differences involved, particularly concerning the Holy Spirit as proceeding from the Father and the Son, the schism was mainly a matter of conflict over Church government and a conflict of personalities.

Today, Eastern Orthodox Christians and Catholics are deeply moved by the desire for unity, as was so evident in the fraternal embrace of the Patriarch Athenagoras and Pope Paul VI. In a significant gesture, they both issued repeals of the mutual excommunication or condemnation promulgated at the time of the great schism. It is the prayer of all that this deep wound in Christian unity may be healed before too long.

Especially important

▶ TO REFLECT ON:

Have you noticed how outstanding some men are, no matter how difficult and confusing the times in which they live? You live in very challenging times. You yourself are already influencing the world around you, perhaps when you least realize it. What kind of a mark are you leaving? Men like King Louis IX or Pope Gregory VII were not made overnight, any more than are the dynamic men of our day. You are shaping your own future—and all those you will influence—*right now*.

▶ TO STRIVE FOR:

You want to develop solid convictions from which nothing will be able to dissuade you, to avoid being whirled about like a weathervane. No pressure or clever saying sways a man or woman whose conduct is based on a clear conviction of the truth taught by Christ and His Church. Strive to be strong in your faith and generous enough to *act on it*.

▶ TO TALK TO GOD ABOUT:

Pray to be numbered among "the greats":
    For ourselves, we ask a place
    with your apostles and martyrs,...
    and all the saints.
    Though we are sinners,
    we trust in Your mercy and love.
    Do not consider what we truly deserve,
    but grant us Your forgiveness
    through Christ our Lord. (Eucharistic Prayer I)

Lord, help me to be bigger than myself.
I haven't got the courage to say what
    I feel about You,
    about helping people.
    I'm afraid of being laughed at.
Still, I have to admit that the times I did really
    let my faith show,
    I was surprised at the way You let
    others find You in me.
Christ Jesus, I want to *affect* people!
I want them to feel I am somebody for Your sake...
Right now, most of the time, no difference shows
    between me and the drifters,...
    Let me realize what a scandal that is!
I want you to help me now, tonight, tomorrow
    there
    and *then*...
to be *You* for somebody.
I want You to help me stand up and be counted
    as one completely given over to You.
    I'm sick of hiding, of doing things only half-way.
    Help me.

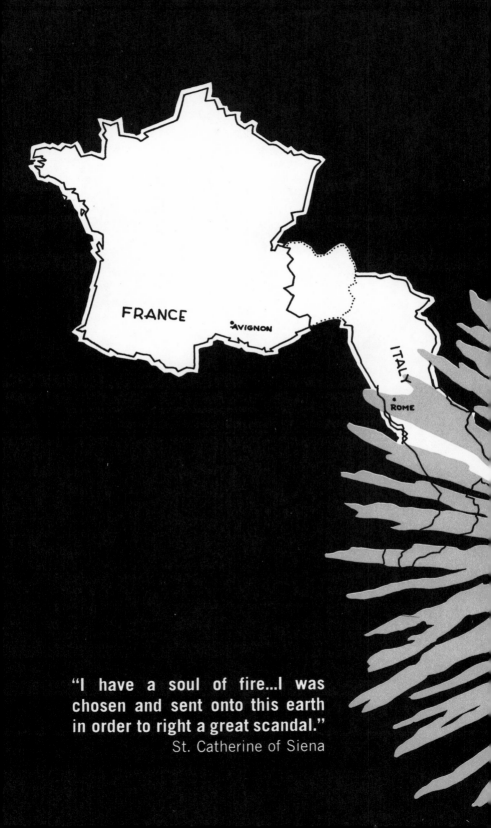

FRANCE

AVIGNON

ITALY

ROME

"I have a soul of fire...I was
chosen and sent onto this earth
in order to right a great scandal."
St. Catherine of Siena

4

A VIBRANT, VIOLENT AGE

F. Messina

"The Church is a house built of our souls.
And this house is not equally respectable
in all its parts.
Among the stones which go to make it up,
some are brilliant and polished,
while others are dark and of inferior quality...."

ST. JOHN CHRYSOSTOM

The threat that heresy constituted, with its accompanying social upheavals, and the steps taken by Church and State to check it, occupy part of the story of this period. These events must be judged in the light of the customs and social climate of the Middle Ages, not by our changed conditions.

The struggle to keep the Church free of control by the greedy brought dramatic conflicts and a long, painful trial. The residence of the Popes in Avignon led to a lessening of their influence and prestige, which was climaxed when three different men all claimed to be Pope. This Western Schism caused great confusion and strife.

On the brighter side, much religious fervor was rekindled by holy men and women, particularly through the religious orders. The new friars, especially the Franciscans and Dominicans, grew rapidly in number and were very successful in checking ignorance, error and vice.

The Middle Ages produced great cathedrals, masterpieces of art, poetry, and music, and world-famous universities. It was a time of rapid progress in the higher studies, especially theology, Sacred Scripture and philosophy.

An old problem with a new name

When the great St. Augustine was young and not yet converted to Christ, he became a follower of a sect known as Manichaeism. Actually, its belief in two gods, one a god of good and the other a god of evil, stretches far back into history. It is easy to see why such a doctrine might at first attract a person, since we all see much goodness and much evil in the world. In looking at the matter further, however, St. Augustine and all deep thinkers realized that there can be only one Supreme Being: if there were two, one would have to have something the other did not, in order to be different, and hence he would no longer be perfect, supreme, infinite.

This old, two-god doctrine showed up again in the twelfth century in southern France. The "new Manichaens" were better known as Cathari ("the purified") or the Albigensians, after the city of Albi, their main center. Because they believed that all material things, even our bodies, are evil, they condemned marriage and held that to bring children into the world was the greatest crime. Life was an evil for them, and suicide by the "Endura," slow starvation, was considered a heroic martyr's death.

"The Perfect" were the higher sect of this new religion, which was bitterly opposed to the Church. Unlike "the Believers," the lower class to which the majority of Albigensians belonged, the Perfect lived lives of chastity, great poverty, fasting, preaching, educating, and dispensing large sums to the needy. They seemed very sincere men and through their zealous efforts, great numbers were converted to the new form of Manichaeism.

By encouraging suicide, complete opposition to birth, and immorality as preferable to marriage, Albigensianism was a great threat to both society and religion. Why did so many accept it?

It would be unfair to lay all the blame on the non-Christians living in southern France who welcomed any chance to encourage rebellion against the Church. Likewise, it would be oversimplifying matters to say that the wealthy, loose-living classes welcomed a sect which taught that there was no purgatory and no hell, that one need only accept the Cathari doctrines and promise to undergo the purification rite called "Consolamentum" before death, being free in the meantime to give into all the passions. These were partial causes, but a very grave cause and a very sinister root of this and other heresies was the state of the average Catholic clergy.

Greed, worldliness, scandalous living and ignorance of religion on the part of many priests, bishops and monks left good people resentful. Sincerely seeking a higher, more spiritual life, many laymen began to take matters into their own hands, and several new movements were started. Some turned to fanatical practices, as did the Flagellants, who scourged themselves in public, or to horrible teachings such as marked the Albigensians; this was due to lack of knowledge of theology and history, and opposition to all authority as established by Christ. Disgusted with some clerics, they turned against the Catholic Church itself. This is a mistake made even in our own day.

Reform certainly was needed, but a reform of men and evil practices, not of the very teachings of Christ. The true reformer begins by reforming himself and, in obedience to Christ's Church, patiently, humbly, perseveringly works to bring about a lasting reform *within* the Church itself. This will be an important factor to remember in studying the Protestant Reformation, for the situation is much the same.

Dominic

Pope Innocent III sent a number of very holy and learned monks to teach the true doctrine of Christ throughout the areas of southern France affected by the Albigensian heresy, as well as neighboring regions of France, of Spain and north Italy. It was a Spanish priest, Dominic de Guzman, however, whom Christ was to make the chief instrument of His cause. St. Dominic founded the Order of Preachers, known as Dominicans. They were dedicated to studying and preaching, in order to stamp out ignorance in religion. Their poverty and penances, too, gave an inspiring example—just what was needed to offset the appeal of the "Perfect" in the erroneous sect. Within sixty years, there were hundreds of Dominican houses, one hundred sixty of which were in the very regions once dominated by the Manichaens.

The Inquisition

Bloody battles were fought over the Albigensian heresy, since part of the reason for its success was the support it received from the chief prince of Languedoc, who held out against his king. Religion was so much a part of the very life of the countries that religious rebellions threw both Church and State into turmoil. The *earthly* and the *eternal* well-being of thousands was at stake.

With these facts in mind, we can understand why the institution known as the *Inquisition* came into being. It was a supreme tribunal, usually composed of monks or friars, by which persons accused of heresy were tried. If they repented of their error, they were reconciled to the Church. If not, they were handed over to the civil authorities, since heresy was considered an offense against the unity and peace of the country. The Inquisition had the power to imprison and fine, but not to impose the death sentence. The civic powers, however, often did put heretics to death.

We moderns, used to friendly co-existence with people of a tremendous variety of religious beliefs or no belief, find it hard to understand why men should have been tried for beliefs. Actually, our own American history is quite full of incidents wherein men of various religions have suffered immensely and have been grievously persecuted because of their creed. The same is true in one country after another.

The heresy of the Albigensians had become a great social threat; moreover, it had become part of the struggle between the various rulers in France. Thus, it was inevitable that a court should be set up to try to end this threat. The Church's part was to examine the defendants, since the civil rulers certainly had no one learned enough in theology to handle the matter.

It was the religious sons of St. Dominic that Pope Gregory IX put in charge of this tribunal empowered to inquire into the existence of heresy. And the Inquisition was successful in stamping out the Manichaen danger.

In 1478, Pope Sixtus IV permitted King Ferdinand and Queen Isabella to set up an Inquisition in Spain. Its goal was to protect the newly united country against the plot of Muslims (Moors) and secret Jews (pretending to be Christians) to overthrow both the government and the Christian religion. Later on, the Spanish Inquisition was directed against the spread of Protestantism.

In those times, all courts used torture and very harsh treatment on defendants. Indeed, the whole penal code was cruel to the extreme. Thus we are shocked at the practices of the Spanish Inquisition, which were most severe. Time and time again, the Pope protested against these methods, but to no avail. In England and France, too, the legal punishments imposed were just as cruel. It was these abuses — which were common to all civil courts of the time — that gave the Inquisition its bad name. Moreover, as in all times of turmoil, undoubtedly more than one sincere, good-willed man suffered. St. Ignatius Loyola himself, founder of the Jesuits, narrowly escaped punishment by the Spanish Inquisition. On the other hand, great numbers were saved from deception in matters of faith, and Christ's truths could again bring them peace and joy in this life and the next.

Dramatic conflicts

The Church lives in the world and is a pilgrim on this earth. At every turn of the road, she faces new struggles, just as every man constantly comes up against both delightful and sorrowful experiences.

We have seen how emperors could be both a help and a hindrance in advancing the cause of Christ. In the Middle Ages, many were definitely a hindrance, and the struggles they brought on were bitter ones.

Two of the most famous involve Henry II of England and Thomas à Becket, Philip IV of France and Pope Boniface VIII.

The key actors in the English drama started out as close friends. Henry II was the most powerful of the English medieval kings. He was a brilliant, capable ruler and recognized the same intelligence, diplomacy and ability in his friend Thomas à Becket, whom he made his chancellor. Later, he nominated Thomas for the highest position in the Church in England: Archbishop of Canterbury. The wily Henry thus planned to be in full control of the revenues of the dioceses and monasteries and to make his own court supreme in Church matters, instead of the Holy See at Rome.

Thomas knew what Henry had in mind, but he also knew that as Archbishop, in conscience, he would have to be loyal to the interests of Christ's Church. So he tried to persuade Henry not to nominate him. Henry thought he knew better. Thomas finally agreed, was ordained a priest, and then bishop. At once, he renounced his luxurious way of life and began devoting his days to prayer, penance and whole-hearted service to God's People.

Just as à Becket had foreseen, the royal friendship soon came to an end. King Henry found that his former chancellor was now a servant of the Church in every fiber of his being. Whereas most of the other bishops gave in to the king's pressure, Archbishop à Becket refused to agree to laws that would have cut the English church off from the Holy Father and the universal Church. Threats, accusations of treason, punishment of the Archbishop's relatives, and the most bitter opposition finally came to a climax when Henry, who was given to fits of violent rage, fumed:

"Of the cowards who eat my bread, is there no one to free me of this turbulent priest?"

Murder in the cathedral

Four knights went to Canterbury, therefore, and cut the Archbishop down right in his cathedral. His last words as he died were, "For the name of Jesus and the defense of the Church, I am ready to die!"

Just three years later, the martyr Thomas à Becket was canonized. His shrine became England's most famous goal of pilgrimages. Chaucer's "Canterbury Pilgrims," of whom every student of English Literature knows, were on their way to St. Thomas' Shrine. The modern English poet and dramatist, T.S. Eliot, wrote a powerful play on the story, called *Murder in the Cathedral,* which has been performed in real cathedrals.

Philip vs. Boniface

Philip IV was a very able, cunning man. Like his grandfather, St. Louis, he was personally likable and devout, but unlike the saint, he was greedy for money and taxed the Church for revenues with which to carry on his wars. He was ready to use anything, from vile slander to downright physical violence on the Pope. Boniface was a learned, strong-willed, elderly man who was determined to protect the rights of religion against such a king. Although he was too stern a man, who acted at times in a very severe manner, he tried hard to be fair and to change Philip's attitude, so as to bring about a peaceful settlement. It is difficult to guess whether any man, even the most winning and lovable, would have been able to soften Philip and his evil advisers, but the fact is that Boniface could not. As a result, he suffered intensely. Still, because of his love for the Church, he never yielded.

The climax came when Philip's men and a band of allies broke into the Pope's residence at Anagni, after being treacherously admitted to the city. Boniface, who knew of their intent, faced them all alone, seated on the papal throne. "Captured by treason like Christ," the courageous old man declared, "I shall die like a Pope." The band grabbed him, treated him offensively and threw him into prison. The people of Anagni finally drove the king's mob out and freed the Pontiff. He died a month later.

In these struggles between Churchmen and kings, the Church often paid dearly, but she had to insist on her freedom from secular control. She had to be loyal to her Divine Founder and to her mission of leading men to God, to a full, rich life in Christ.

The "Babylonian Captivity"

The Popes of the twelfth and thirteenth centuries had spent much time in many different towns and cities of Italy for one reason or another. But from 1309 to 1376, the papacy resided permanently at Avignon, which was located in territory belonging to the papacy yet connected only by a bridge to French soil. When the move was first made, it was not intended to be permanent. The fighting going on in Rome and throughout Italy, where the Pope's temporal power existed in name only, kept the Avignon Popes from returning.

To the people, it seemed as though Peter had deserted his city, as though the Pope had made the Church French, an ally of the French king. This is why the Avignon period was called the "Babylonian Captivity," recalling the period in Old Testament when God's Chosen People were held captive in the pagan city of Babylon. The fact is, however, that all the Avignon Popes were universal in outlook, sent out missionaries as the Church has always done, and in many affairs showed clearly their independence from French imperial policies.

The Popes who lived at Avignon were always Bishops of Rome (that fact is what made them Popes — successors of St. Peter in his Bishopric of Rome). They only lived at Avignon....

Yet, as Daniel-Rops has said, "The absence of the papacy from Rome seemed treason to Christendom.... The holy city... could not remain the widow to St. Peter's successor." From all over rose voices pleading for the return of the Pontiff to Rome.

Catherine of Siena

It was St. Catherine of Siena, the indomitable woman of God, who was instrumental in bringing Pope Gregory XI back to Rome. This dynamic mystic wielded incredible influence in Siena and other cities of Italy, making peace between the warring parties, fighting for the interests of the Church, urging princes, princesses and Popes to rally to the cause of Christ with greater dedication. Though she could neither read nor write, she had so won a band of priests, monks and laymen that they acted as her secretaries and ambassadors, and strove to imitate her astounding holiness and union with God.

In person, Catherine went to Pope Gregory at Avignon and convinced him that God willed the return to Rome. Then when he died at Rome and Urban VI was elected, she foresaw the trouble his stern ways and very harsh methods would bring. Writing to him with the greatest respect, calling him the "sweet Christ on earth," she nevertheless exhorted him to soften his treatment of his cardinals. In vain! As a result, the humiliated, furious cardinals declared his election invalid and elected "another Pope," who went to live at Avignon.

The great Western Schism had begun. The Christian world was faced with the spectacle of "two Popes"! Before it all ended forty years later, there would be three men claiming to be the true Pope! No wonder Catherine, the ardent lover of the Church, died tormented by a prophetic vision of this disaster. The vision caused her to keep murmuring, "Blood! Blood!" The times were indeed times of great turmoil and suffering for the Mystical Body, the Bride of Christ, as well as for civil society.

St. Catherine,
advisor of princes and Popes

"Three Popes" at one time...

Since there was such confusion as to who was the true Pope, many dioceses had two men claiming to be bishop. Saintly people were to be found among the supporters of both the Rome and Avignon claimants. Division and strife was the order of the day, and as a result, evil practices in the Church grew. In addition, wars were going on in many countries and the plague called the Black Death was killing countless numbers, particularly among the better clergy who were generously tending the sufferers. All these factors contributed to the alarming unrest that clouded the scene.

How did the three-pope schism end? A council of bishops was convened, and the Pope at Rome, Gregory XII, later agreed to recognize it as a general or ecumenical council and then to resign. The Emperor Sigismund forced one of the other "popes" to resign, and the third one had lost all his followers by this time. The council now elected a new Pope, and the great schism was ended. The Church had once again come through the storm, through the power of Christ, her Head, who never abandons her.

A new problem had come into being with the ending of the schism, however, and that was the "conciliar problem." Some people now felt that a general council was superior to a Pope. Moreover, since the parliaments were becoming stronger in authority in several countries, these churchmen wanted to see the Church run on a "parliamentary basis," forgetting that Christ, the head of the Church had entrusted supreme power to His Vicar. Ecumenical councils of bishops exercise supreme authority only together with the Pope and never without him.

Attempts were made in the following decades to run general councils without the Supreme Pontiff, but they all failed, and the "conciliar problem" came to an end.

Stunning images of Christ

The Middle Ages can boast of some unforgettable men and women who imaged Christ in spectacular if unconventional ways. We have seen Thomas à Becket, the courtier who became the Church's champion; Dominic, the gentle hammer of heretics; and Catherine of Siena, the merchant's daughter who turned ambassador to princes and Popes. There are many more, perhaps the best known of whom is St. Francis of Assisi. Indeed, the religious orders were fertile beds of extraordinary holiness in those times, as they had been since the earliest days of the Church.

Religious life is a special way of following Christ, of witnessing to Him; it is a closer imitation of His own life of poverty, chastity and obedience, of wholehearted service of God and man. We read of consecrated virgins in the very first centuries, such as Saints Agnes, Cecilia and Dorothy. Later, certain men began leaving familiar surroundings for lives of solitude and prayer, the better to study Christ, to adore Him, to pray and do penance for their brethren. They were known as *Anchorites*. As places of solitude became harder to find, and as the persecution raged more fiercely, many men took refuge in desert areas. St. Paul of the Desert and St. Anthony were the most famous of these desert *hermits*.

Women also dared to live the life of solitude and penance, as for instance, St. Mary of Egypt, a beautiful, immoral caravan follower who was converted and at last found inner peace and joy in doing penance for her loose life.

St. Pachomius was the first solitary to draw hermits together to live in monasteries under a common rule and under a superior. He was undoubtedly inspired by the words of Christ: "Wherever two or three are gathered in my name, there am I in their midst." Women also formed communities, and convents of nuns arose.

Aiming at still greater perfection in this life of work and prayer, St. Basil, the illustrious Eastern Father, advised the men and women religious to take the vows of poverty, chastity, and obedience, to be more like the Christ of the Gospel — poor, virginal, and wholly obedient to His Father's will.

In the West, as we have seen, St. Benedict was the founder of *monasticism*. The Benedictine way of life became the rule in nearly all European monasteries. But from the time of Charlemagne on, besides monks, there had also been *canons regular*, who combined the monastic life with priestly duties in parishes.

The Middle Ages saw new, dynamic orders of canons being founded by holy men of vision like St. Norbert. The Benedictines were renewed in fervor through the Cluny reform, as we saw. A new form of the ancient hermits' life was the Carthusian order, founded by St. Bruno. Carthusians even today live alone, each in his own hut, to which is attached

St. Bernard, devoted son of Mary

the garden he cultivates. The huts are close to one another and there is one church for all. They are guided and governed by a hermit-abbot, to avoid the excesses and fanaticism which marked some of the ancient solitaries. For human nature being what it is, we all have need of understanding and guidance, to avoid deceiving ourselves — something that is very easy to do in spiritual matters.

The rugged men of Clairvaux

The best-known order founded in the Middle Ages is the Cistercian Order. The lives and struggles of the Englishman, St. Stephen Harding, and St. Bernard, two of its early abbots, make good reading, indeed. Silence and self-sacrifice for *love* mark this life meant for men rugged in body and soul.

The Cistercian, Bernard of Clairvaux, had such incredible influence on the mid-twelfth century that this period is often called the "Age of St. Bernard." Like Catherine of Siena, Bridget of Sweden, Patrick of Ireland and a host of others, Bernard was gifted with the highest contemplative prayer and was also a man of tremendous activity. He wrote numerous works on theology and mysticism, he preached, he counseled rulers of Church and State, he organized. He was the implacable foe of the Church's bitter enemies as well as the ardent author of joyous, confident prayers and hymns, especially to the beloved Mother of God. The power of his personality was such that once he had spoken on an issue, his word was accepted.

In the career of St. Bernard, we have proof once again of the way a man who renounces ambition and power is raised by God to positions of untold influence on the lives of millions. God seldom makes what we would call "logical choices" when picking His champions, but they all have one thing in common: they hold nothing back in their commitment to Him.

Francis and the friars

What picture does the name of Francis of Assisi bring to mind? Regrettably, many think of cute little statues of a brown-robed fellow with birds on his shoulder, decorating a garden bird-bath. Those who know more recall his conversion from a totally frivolous life as the pampered son of a wealthy merchant to a beggar for Christ's sake. But this is still far from an adequate idea of the meaning of Francis in Church History.

Christ, who founded the Church, has never left it. It is as much His now as it was when He carefully, prayerfully established it, taking pains to train its leaders. He is as interested in the people of one century as in those of another. Hence, for every new development in the world — that world that is also His and beloved by Him — He provides new initiatives, new spiritual undertakings to meet people where they are and in what they need.

In the High Middle Ages, there were new developments: much more wealth and its accompanying evils; growth of cities for whom the priests were too few and the monks located too far out in the countryside; new missionary opportunities among non-Christians that required societies of men not tied down to any one area. The *friars* were the answer to these needs.

Dominic's men were friars, as were the followers of Francis. Francis himself was at first primarily concerned with giving a witness of Gospel poverty and of complete detachment from wealth and convenience. The monks had to own vast estates for the support of their many good works, and their labor and charity was their apostolate, but Francis wanted his men to offset the universal greed of the times by owning *nothing*, depending for their needs on what they received by begging. It took an iron will on Francis' part to embrace stark poverty, to accept insults and the staggering humiliation involved in begging at the wealthy homes in which he had once been the life of the party. He let no protest from his human nature stop him, however, and his followers multiplied by leaps and bounds.

Francis of Assisi: the troubador who became Christ's beggar

Both the Franciscan and Dominicans, as well as the other major orders of friars—the Carmelites and Augustinians—traveled from village to village, city to city, preaching and teaching, living in humble poverty, united in obedience to their local and general superiors. They also dedicated themselves to higher studies, to theology and philosophy, so as to be able to remedy the dreadful religious ignorance of the great masses of the people and to lift the level of learning among the clergy, too.

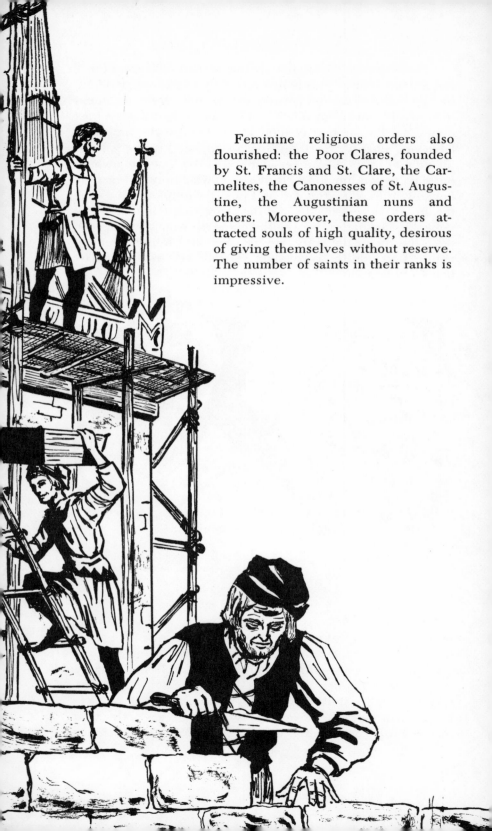

Feminine religious orders also flourished: the Poor Clares, founded by St. Francis and St. Clare, the Carmelites, the Canonesses of St. Augustine, the Augustinian nuns and others. Moreover, these orders attracted souls of high quality, desirous of giving themselves without reserve. The number of saints in their ranks is impressive.

Medieval masterpieces

Masterpieces came into being in this vibrant period, not only in human personalities, but in art and architecture, in theology and philosophy, in poetry and music. As in the case of the fascinating personalities, these masterpieces are studied today with as much interest and pleasure as ever.

Art and architecture's greatest boast of the period is the celebrated Gothic cathedral. The style had been the sturdy, rugged one called romanesque, but around 1150 the high vaulted roofs and flying buttresses of the Gothic style began to appear. Besides their awesome height, in which the human spirit seems to find space and breath to soar, these masterpieces of architecture offered glorious artwork in their brilliant stained-glass windows, statues and paintings. The various truths of faith were all there before the eyes of the people, so that although they could neither read nor write, the great mysteries of the faith were vividly impressed on their minds.

Moving Latin hymns were composed, such as the *Salve Regina* (Hail, Holy Queen) and the *Adoro Te Devote* (Humbly We Adore You). Dante Alighieri wrote the most famous masterpiece of all medieval poetry, *The Divine Comedy,* which is undoubtedly one of the world's greatest epic poems. It is an allegorical account of the poet's imaginary journey through hell, purgatory and heaven. No one who reads it can forget it, so vivid are the scenes he paints with words. Scholars pour over it tirelessly, ever finding new, richer meanings in the symbolism. Only a combination of rare genius and deep faith could have produced *The Divine Comedy.*

Search for truth

In the exciting search for learning, the Middle Ages gave rise to marvelous universities in England, France, Spain and Italy. They were Catholic in every sense of the word, for many were directly under the Holy Father's authority, and all were Church-sponsored; moreover, their students came from all over Europe. More important, the spirit of discovery, of a relentless quest for knowledge made them exciting places in which to study.

Dante and his "Divine Comedy"

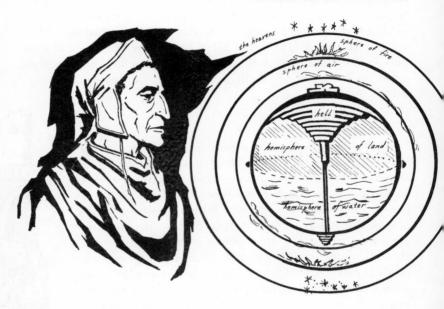

Theology held first place, but philosophy soon became almost as important and toward the end of the period, the natural sciences and scientific methods were coming into their own, particularly through the work of the Franciscan friar, Roger Bacon. Outstanding minds met and often confronted one another. Indeed, controversy became heated at times. Some of the most famous of the intellectual stars of this period are St. Thomas Aquinas, St. Albert the Great, St. Bonaventure, St. Anselm, Abelard, Peter Lombard and John Duns Scotus.

Thomas Aquinas is often thought of as a huge, placid man who sat in calm silence and wrote his monumental *Summa*

Theologica, his *Summa Contra Gentiles* and other works, without a ripple of opposition. The fact is that Thomas' ideas were considered daring; he was called upon to defend himself publicly before the Bishop of Paris; and even after his death, it took some years before his fellow Dominicans succeeded in clearing his name and reputation of the charge of error. We could say in general that this mastermind, who was also an extremely holy, witty, wonderful man, wrote the greatest explanation of the truths known both by *faith* and by *reason. The trouble came because he used Aristotle,* the most important philosopher of the ancient world.

Thomas and the Golden Age

It was the Arabs of the Mohammedan Empire who first "re-discovered" Aristotle, and at once men took sides when it

The wisdom of the Greeks and Arabs
reached a climax in the genius
of Thomas Aquinas

came to the genius' religious ideas. There was no problem involved in his rules for right thinking (called the science of logic) or in his defense of our mind's ability to arrive at truth (called the science of epistemology) or in other branches of his thought. But the question was what Aristotle thought about God, creation and the immortality of the human soul. One Arab philosopher, Averroes interpreted Aristotle as denying these truths, which set him in opposition to Islam's teachings. The Jewish philosophers in Spain who interpreted Aristotle faced the same problem.

It was through the Arab and Jewish commentators that Aristotelianism reached the Catholic University of Paris, and it is understandable that twice it was forbidden to teach Aristotle. It soon came to be known, however, that if one read Aristotle's work in the Greek, without the Averroistic interpretations, the picture changed. In fact, St. Thomas *used* Aristotle's historic achievements in thinking to set forth the deepest truths and to give a solid natural support to truths revealed by religion. In his genius, he "corrects" or "fills in" points that the Greek philosopher, unaided by the wisdom of Christianity, could not know. For his learning and holiness Thomas Aquinas is called the "Angelic Doctor."

Thus was born the period of learning known as *The Golden Age of Scholasticism*. Quite differently from our times, when colleges and universities give forth uncertain opinions on the basic areas of life and learning, the schoolmen of this period saw reason and faith joined to build up a great body of truth, mankind's precious heritage.

Especially important

▶ TO REFLECT ON:

Handicaps are sometimes our excuse for doing "nothing big." We say we don't have the time, or the talent, or the right friends, or the brains, or the money, or the "breaks," or the social class, or the physical stength.... A girl says: "If only I were a man" — but she forgets St. Catherine of Siena. A boy says: "If only I didn't have to worry about what my friends will say," — but he forgets Thomas à Becket, whose friend-turned-enemy was none other than a powerful king. Ask yourself what reasons you give for not being more Christ-like, more involved in doing good, more firm morally and spiritually. Examine those reasons honestly. Are they really *good* reasons?

▶ TO STRIVE FOR:

Having decided what you ought to do, in a positive way, to open up to God's grace stirring in you, resolve not to slip back into the old, easy but unsatisfying way. Let the real you speak your convictions. Stand your ground, trusting joyfully in Christ's love for you and in your ability to *give* joy to others. Resolve to let this dominate your efforts, your relationships with others, your moments of success and even of defeat.

▶ TO TALK TO GOD ABOUT:

Lord, give me the strength
to be ready always to serve
    those around me.
Let me willingly do more than the minimum
    so I'll be sure of not doing too little.
Let me be the first to be where the work is,
    ready to do the messy jobs,
    to let somebody else have it easier.
Just give me the chance
    to grow in You by giving of myself to everybody,
    starting with my own family.
Don't let me sell myself or You or Your Church to be
    popular.
Let me make other people happy,
    but never at the expense of saddening You.

Pray the *Our Father* slowly, for all the People of God, with your heart open especially to the weak, the sinful, the bewildered.

5

BREAK—UP

"If it were possible to see men's souls laid bare, we should find in the Church, as in an army after a battle, that some are dead and others wounded.

"So, then, I beg and pray you, let us lend one another a hand to rise again."

St. John Chrysostom

Even in the beginnings
of the one and only Church of God,
there arose certain rifts,
which the Apostle strongly condemned.
But in subsequent centuries much more serious
dissensions made their appearance,
and quite large Communities came to be "separated"
from full communion with the Catholic Church—
for which, often enough,
"men of both sides were to blame."

DECREE ON ECUMENISM, VATICAN II

After surveying the extent of Christendom at the dawn of the Renaissance period, this chapter looks at the conditions of that Christendom to determine the causes leading up to the revolt against the Church in the sixteenth century. We have already seen attempts at needed reform, but evil conditions persisted and the explosive situation was intensified by political events.

The main figures in the break with the Church are Martin Luther and John Calvin. The role of Henry VIII and Elizabeth I in the development of Protestantism are also to be considered.

Bright and dark sides of the picture

Although the prophetic vision of the Sienese saint Catherine revealed all too clearly the trials ahead, outwardly, the Church looked strong and prosperous at the end of the fourteenth century. Geographically, Christendom included all northern, western, central and Mediterranean Europe. Some of the later countries to be converted, namely Hungary and Poland, had proven very staunch in the faith. Indeed, Poland had been a strong supporter of Pope Gregory VII in his struggle with Henry IV. Again, it was through the Polish princess Hedwig that Lithuania had turned definitively to Christ in the latter part of the fourteenth century. In Scandinavia, where St. Anschar had labored so successfully, Denmark and Norway had become Catholic countries in the eleventh century. Thus Europe could be called Christian, although the threat of the Ottoman Turks, who had conquered Asia Minor, was ever present.

Even in Asia, moreover, Christianity was being slowly planted; successful beginnings had been made in Persia and in distant China.

But despite the vast area claimed by Christianity and the imposing structures of her well-organized government, her gorgeous cathedrals built by the joint, loving efforts of rich and poor alike, her huge abbeys and monasteries, universities and schools; despite the deep, if sometimes misguided, fervor that prompted endless pilgrimages and enthusiastic displays of devotion — despite all this evidence of faith, there was the darker side of the picture, which we must examine with honesty.

In addition to the many devout, learned clergy who went about their duties as loyal, zealous servants of Christ and His Church, there were those who scandalized everyone by their lack of virtue, their greed, their unchaste lives, their total indifference to the things of the spirit. Many a priest publicly lived with a woman as though she were his wife, and thought more of maneuvering his children into rich, powerful positions than of the state of his immortal soul, or the souls of his flock, and their needs.

It must be remembered that there were no such institutions as seminaries in those times. The universities which taught theology, philosophy, Scripture and the other bodies of knowledge came to be, in many cases, corrupting influences. To see why, we have to look into the movement called the *Renaissance,* which means "rebirth."

97

The Renaissance

The Renaissance began in Italy, and was a reawakened admiration and imitation of the ancient Greek and Roman classics in art and literature. Italy was filled with men passionately devoted to ideals of creative beauty. This is the age of the incomparable artists Michelangelo, Leonardo da Vinci, and Raphael, whose magnificent religious paintings and statues are considered among the world's priceless treasures. Men were eagerly studying Plato, Cicero, and all the literary masters of the ancient Greeks and Romans. From Italy, the

Michelangelo produced his Pieta at the age of twenty-five.

Renaissance was to sweep through Germany, France, and later still, through England, giving us men of the genius of Shakespeare.

The thoroughly pagan influence, however, that accompanied the "worship" of classical Greece and Rome was not a good thing for the morals of the people. Emphasis on the sensual pleasures tended to lead to imitation of the immorality found in much of this literature, and thus the situation among university students can be imagined.

So great was the accent on the external marks of religion, on gorgeous decorations, on stupendous statues and paintings, that Renaissance Popes and civil rulers competed with one another for the services of the famous artists. People "wore" their religion in high style, but in many cases, particularly among the poorly-instructed, simple folk, much of this religion was external only, and much was absolute superstition. For example, completely false "relics" were widely sold like good luck charms by unscrupulous men.

Reform was greatly needed, but the Church's reformatory program reached its supreme success only after the Church had been weakened and grieved by a painful break.

The sad state of the Renaissance Papacy

With so much spiritual strength at her command and so many holy people crying for reform, why was it that the Church could not shake off the crippling evils? In 1522, Pope Adrian VI openly declared the reason, the reason that everyone had been saying, some sadly and some with violent fury:

"We know well that for many years there have come forth also from this Holy See itself many despicable things: abuses of spiritual things, transgressions of commandments. *Indeed, in everything, there has been a turn for the worse.* Therefore, it is not surprising that the illness has transplanted itself from the head to the members, from the popes to the hierarchy."

"A turn for the worse" — when Roderigo Borgia became Pope Alexander VI, matters definitely went from bad to worse. Before him, there had been scandals in the Vatican, as popes made their young nephews cardinals solely to build up their family fortunes, and some of these young men lived riotously and immorally. Wild parties, intrigues, bribery and simony were not unusual, for there were too many wealthy, aristocratic clerics who looked on high positions in only one light: opportunities for more wealth and power.

Even a man such as Pope Julius II, stern and austere, gave scandal because of his passion for political conquests, which induced him actually to wield a war club at the head of his armies! He and some other Renaissance popes patronized the glorious artistic creations of the Renaissance to the neglect of energetic reform.

But Alexander VI was the source of the greatest scandal of all, not only because of the illegitimate children he had when elected, but because he continued his sinful life even as Pope, and because he publicly bestowed honors and positions on his two favorite children, Cesare and Lucrezia. Cesare was particularly infamous; he would stop at nothing to promote his ambitions. That Holy Church, the Bride of the God-Man, could be at the mercy of such ruthless people and still survive is indeed astonishing! Yet survive she did, for Christ's divine power never leaves His Church.

Moreover, although his personal life makes us think of the words of Jesus: "Scandals must come, but woe to him through whom they come!" — still, the fair historian has to admit that in his official actions, Pope Alexander VI never worked against the interests of the Church, against her true teachings on faith or morals. Obviously, the Holy Spirit was still protecting her from error, despite the weak human being at her head.

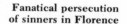

**Fanatical persecution
of sinners in Florence**

The tragedy of Savonarola

In Florence, a small, shrivelled little monk named Jerome Savonarola whipped crowds to fever pitch by his pas-

sionate preaching of the message: the Bride of Christ is tainted
with sin and must be purified. He was convinced that he was
a prophet sent from God, and the Florentines believed him.
The wealthy gave back money unjustly earned, women gave
up jewels, artists destroyed their pagan-inspired works. But
Savonarola let his enthusiasm turn to excess: bands of men
were allowed to go through the streets "persecuting sinners"
to the point where terror ruled the city. When the monk's
political allies, the French, were chased out of Florence, the
people began to rebel against the violent rule of Savonarola.
Soon he fell from power and was burned at the stake. The
tragedy of this man is that he had good intentions and the
cause of reform desperately needed his great preaching
ability, but his mission was ruined by his violence, political
ambitions and attack not only on the evil man who was Pope
(Alexander VI) but also on his authority as Pope.

Joan of Arc—patriot

Who has not heard of *Joan of Arc*, the warrior-maid of
Orleans? Her mysterious Voices from heaven, the voices of
St. Michael, St. Margaret and St. Catherine, commanded her:
"Leave your village, daughter of God, and journey into
France! Choose your standard and raise it boldly! You shall
deliver France from the English!" Obediently she went to
battle "in the name of the King of heaven," to make her beloved homeland a free nation again. The people rallied to
her, convinced of her supernatural mission and fired by her
own patriotism.

The life of Joan of Arc, then, shows us clearly how the
countries of Christendom were thinking of themselves more
and more as separate, sovereign nations. The *national spirit*
was on the rise, even though the dream of a united Christendom, unscarred by internal wars, was deeply rooted in Joan,
as it had been in Catherine of Siena. The same is true of
Ferdinand and Isabella of Spain.

When the beautiful blonde Princess Isabella of Castile
chose Prince Ferdinand of Aragon as her husband, a divided
Spain was set on the path to unification. As queen, she rode
with him and their armies to reclaim the region of Spain still
ruled by the Moslems. The faith and devotion of this renowned queen matched her courage. Though passionately

dedicated to the newly unified country, she envisioned winning new nations for Christ and enlarging His earthly kingdom. It was the "Catholic Sovereigns," Ferdinand and Isabella, who financed the famous voyage of Christopher Columbus in 1492. Spain was to become one of the greatest Christian nations, firmly united in devotion to Christ, to His Church, and to its Christian rulers, and very influential in spreading the faith in the New World.

The vibrant nationalism so evident in Spain and France was also strong in England and in Germany. But it contained dangers. Some kings and politicians would use the disgust with Roman scandals to win followers for their plans to dominate completely the Church and the papacy. Failing in this, their final resort was to throw off obedience to the papacy and to make themselves the lay-popes of national churches separated from Rome.

Love of God and country shown in France's Joan and Spain's Ferdinand and Isabella

Leading up to revolt

We have looked into a number of causes of the revolt soon to come under the leadership of Martin Luther, John Calvin, John Knox, and King Henry VIII. Reform, we recognize, was truly needed, even though the evil, being sensational, certainly did much to obscure the vast numbers of saintly priests, religious and laity. We could name St. Catherine of Bologna, daughter of an ambassador; Blessed Amadeus IX, Duke of Savoy; St. Lawrence Justinian, the noble Archbishop of Venice; St. John Capistrano, St. Catherine of Genoa, St. Antoninus of Florence, St. Francis of Paola — all belonging to the century preceding the Reformation. The great popularity of the Bible, of devotional books and catechisms, the great crowds praying fervently at the shrines — all tell a much brighter story about the deep faith of the vast majority.

Moreover, the doctrine of the Church, as taught even by the unworthy Popes, had remained sound. Not one erroneous doctrine had been issued. No heresies appeared during the Renaissance period. Before that time, however, there had been two important ones.

One had been that of the Englishman John Wycliffe, who rejected the papacy, the priesthood, the sacraments, and especially the doctrine of transubstantiation: the teaching that Christ is really, truly and substantially present in the Eucharist. Another attack had been made by John Hus of Bohemia, whose ideas influenced Luther, especially his teaching that faith *alone,* not good works on our part, is the means of salvation.

The private agony of Martin Luther

It is no easy task to understand the anguished, fiery soul of Martin Luther. The inner drama of this man, whose bright eyes and expressive hands revealed the restlessness and power of his nature, was to become the drama of a religious upheaval.

The first thirty-four years of his life were quite ordinary and outwardly calm. In the judgment of his fellow students, he was not only a brilliant student, but a good, friendly companion. After his entrance into the Augustinian Order, he was esteemed as a fervent friar. He became extremely popular and successful as a teacher of theology and a preacher.

Martin Luther did not
show the despair he felt

Underneath all this, however, Martin Luther was living his own private agony. He kept believing himself damned. No matter what he tried — prayer, penance, fasting, even daily confession — his despair did not leave him. He could not seem to cling to the fact of God's great love for us. No one can say for sure what made him live in such terror; some feel it was a mental or emotional problem.

In the midst of this spiritual torture, Luther hit upon the doctrine that was to give him relief: we are saved by faith alone, so we do not have to try to repent, perform good actions or progress in virtue. This doctrine was in conflict with Christian teaching, which says that Christ did indeed redeem us but that because He has given us a free will, we must cooperate with His saving grace and, by acts of repentance and charity, make an effort to resemble Him.

On All Saints' eve, 1517, Luther posted a list of ninety-five propositions on the church door in Wittenburg, Germany, where he was teaching, and prepared to defend his new ideas. Reacting against the abuses in the practice of granting indulgences, he declared also that the Church could not grant them at all.

In the next few years, his charges against the Church became even more radical. When asked to retract his errors, he refused, but even two years after hurling forth his challenge, he still declared to the Pope: "Before God and man, I have never wished to attack either the Roman Church or Your Holiness, and today I have even less intention of doing so."

Yet he went further and further down the road to a break with the Church, mainly because there were many in Germany anxious to use him as a tool of their ambitions or personal hatreds.

The papacy had to take a strong stand against Luther's doctrines. Some of the papal agents were unfit to handle the problem. But this was not true of Cardinal Cajetan, the reformer of the Dominican Order. He was perhaps the greatest theologian of his order after St. Thomas Aquinas. Cardinal Cajetan was kind to Luther, but after Luther refused to submit, the cardinal, too, had to take a strong hand.

Luther defiantly burned the papal decree which excommunicated him, even though he had expressed sorrow at his condemnation. This curious combination of melancholy and violence was typical of the man. He had a yearning for genuine piety, but not too deep an understanding of theology.

To save his life, Luther had to go into hiding. Germany was divided on the question. Some people were against him; others felt he was a champion of reform. Luther himself made it clear that reform of scandals was not as important to him as the spiritual problem of salvation by faith, his own personal problem. In hiding, he was again tortured by doubts and fears. He managed, however, to produce his German translation of the New Testament.

Seventeen other German translations had already been printed and there were around a hundred in manuscript form, but Luther's style was so simple and clear that housewives, children, and businessmen could enjoy it, as he himself said. Three thousand copies were sold out in three months!

What were some of Luther's ideas which were being printed and widely circulated in pamphlet form? He rejected all the sacraments except Baptism and the Holy Eucharist (and his ideas about the Holy Eucharist were quite different — he rejected the Mass); he rejected the teaching authority of the Pope, and the ordained priesthood. He declared that the sole guide in religion is the Bible. In particular he urged the

German princes to break with Rome and seize the wealthy properties of the Church for themselves.

Luther, a mystifying contradiction

What many of Luther's followers wanted, more than reform, was a German Church, and Luther was moved by their desires. Thus, his religious movement rapidly became, in great part, a national, political movement. In fact, once it gained speed, events slipped out of his control, which was a source of great bitterness to him. He found himself having to change his message and his allegiance with the quick succession of events.

The peasants had rallied to him, thinking his doctrine supported their desire for freedom, but when they revolted and rioted, a horrified Luther urged the princes to exterminate them, which they did, literally. Over this tragedy, Luther suffered for the rest of his life.

Again, at first he had said that the Church was purely spiritual, invisible, but later he changed his position and said it had to be visible, organized, subject to a hierarchy.

On·marriage, though he abandoned his habit and his vows, he at first had no intention of marrying. Four years later, he married Katherine von Bora, an ex-Cistercian nun, but the marriage seemed to be for him a source of embarrassment and humiliation.

Martin Luther was indeed a mystifying contradiction: sometimes quite vulgar and coarse in speech and writing, sometimes poetic and tender in his religious hymns—as in the ever popular *Away in a Manger*, sometimes incredibly violent, sometimes warm and gentle. He used his great gifts as a speaker and writer to inspire faith as well as to bestow coarse names on the hated Pope. There is no question but that he was a powerful personality, and at the same time a moving, tragic figure.

Germany was in turmoil, with Catholic and Lutheran princes lined up against each other. Attempts were made to bring peace, but the final outcome of a compromise, called the Peace of Augsburg was that Lutheranism was to enjoy equal rights with Catholicism; the religion chosen by the prince of a region was to decide the religion of all his people! This last fact made the political rulers also supreme in religious affairs!

Fourteen years after Luther's break, Denmark, Norway and Sweden were Lutheran, due to their rulers.

Conflict within Protestantism

Even in Luther's own lifetime, various forms of Protestantism developed, which greatly worried and angered him. Ulrich *Zwingli* made true religion consist simply of the Scriptures, interpreted by each individual, but this practical Swiss built up a state church, joining politics to religion. An ex-priest, he himself married, and he had all religious houses closed. His religion spread, amid scenes of burning and destruction, to other parts of Switzerland, but many areas remained faithful to Catholicism, and civil war followed between the two divisions.

A compromise between Lutheranism and Zwinglianism best describes the religion practiced at Basle, while in the city of Strasbourg, an ex-Dominican named *Bucer* tried to bring some unity to Protestantism, already so sharply divided. Bucer rejected Luther's idea of "believe and do what you want, for as long as you feel sure that Christ has redeemed you, you will be saved."

On the sacrament of Holy Eucharist, also, the various groups of Protestants were radically opposed to each other. Zwingli, for example, rejected the Real Presence of our Lord in the Eucharist. Luther, instead, while confessing that he would have liked to reject this doctrine in order to direct a real blow at "the Papists," still felt that the Gospel made it very plain that Christ is really present in the bread and wine. However, he felt that the Lord is really there *only* during the act of reception; the bread and wine still remain according to him.

Despair and violent anger filled Luther at the spectacle of ever-increasing disunity. "It would be better to announce eternal damnation than salvation after the style of Zwingli...," he declared.

Sincere Protestants and Catholics alike suffered greatly because no real reform of morals had taken place in either group. Religion was more mixed up with politics than ever. Worst of all, the unity which Christ had so strongly stressed was disastrously broken. The Mystical Body was afflicted by an open wound which all sincere Christians today are courageously trying to heal.

It was the second greatest Protestant leader, John Calvin, who frankly and sorrowfully confessed: "It is ridiculous beyond measure that, having broken with everyone, we should from the very beginning of our own reform agree so little among ourselves."

John Calvin, cold intellectual

Calvin has been called "the icy genius" because of his severe, cold manner, which made him so different from the fiery Luther. He founded in Geneva a form of Protestantism in which the state was subject to the Church. Calvin was the absolute ruler in Geneva, to which he had fled from France.

John Calvin does not seem to have been so spiritually tormented as Martin Luther, although he, too, was bothered about the problem of salvation or damnation. In answering that, Calvin set forth his doctrine of *Predestination*. This doctrine teaches that we do not have free will, and there is nothing we can do about our salvation; before we are born, God has already decided whether each of us is to be saved or damned. Nothing a man does can change that, said Calvin.

Speaking of this theory of his, he himself declared: "I confess that this statement is quite horrible." It is even worse when we realize that he thought only a few people were among the elect, the saved ones.

**John Calvin used his writing talent
to spread his new religion**

Calvin's first experience with the people of Geneva was so unsuccessful that he was forcefully expelled. This was a dark period for him as his health was poor, and he was in anguish of spirit. But later the Genevans asked him to return, and he became supreme ruler there, in both the political and spiritual fields. From the schools he set up in Geneva, missionaries were trained to spread the new doctrine to France, Holland, Scotland, England and the other parts of Europe.

Through John Knox, Calvin's most famous pupil, Scotland became Calvinist, but here the religion was called Presbyterianism. In Holland it was called the Dutch Reformed Church. In France, Calvinists were called Huguenots, but France, as well as Poland and Hungary, remained largely Catholic. The Puritans who came to America from England practiced a form of Calvinism, too.

Calvin as a writer and church founder

John Calvin intended to set up a counter-church opposed to Catholicism, and for this reason, he used his very logical mind and his marvelous talents as a writer to formulate and popularize a clear body of teachings, in language the ordinary people of the day could grasp and remember. He worked hard and long at his writing, despite his sickly, wasted body. The most famous of his works is the *Christian Institution,* which he published in Latin and in French. There was also a small size edition, just seven by four inches, which could be hidden in the pocket, and this little volume played a major role in spreading Calvinism. Indeed, in the sixteenth century, no other book was so popular. Calvin was, beyond doubt, a far better writer than Luther. The *Christian Institution* provided Protestants with a clear, forceful exposition of a faith, even though most of the later adherents of Calvinism changed various aspects of this doctrine.

Luther lamented the fact that people were abusing his teaching and using it as an excuse to live immorally. Calvinists, instead, were very concerned to do good works, live a good, upright, honest life *to show* that they were among the predestined, the saved. A mark of being a chosen soul was faith, and faith was proved by a good life. Moreover, to be prosperous, they thought, was obviously a sign of God's blessing and pleasure; therefore, wealth, used well and with gratitude to God, was a mark of a good moral man. Poor people, instead, felt doubly crushed: by misery in this life and the prospect of damnation in the next!

Another mark of Calvinism was lack of joyousness in religion, of warm color and enthusiasm; indeed, even in everyday life, the lighter, merrier side of human existence such as recreation, was frowned upon. There would be no room here for the humor and wit of a St. Philip Neri, who was one of the Catholic reformers, or the joy of a St. Francis of Assisi, who delighted in sharing the poverty of Christ. Humility and an all-forgiving love of enemies were two other Gospel virtues which John Calvin could not find it in his heart to practice.

A brilliant mind, a strong will to draw up a new church forever sealed off from the Church of his baptism, a tremendous capacity to work despite severe pain—these were Calvin's qualities. When he died at fifty of tuberculosis, the rupture in Christian unity was greater than ever.

Henry VIII and Anne Boleyn

Protestantism in England cannot boast of leaders of the type of Luther and Calvin; indeed, there arises the temptation to say that it was born of an unlawful love affair. This, however, would be too simple an explanation, for it is undeniable that the same ills of ignorance, greed, and unscrupulous politics all had a part to play in the final results.

As a young monarch, Henry VIII was considered one of the most handsome and accomplished rulers in Europe. He was devout, well-educated, athletic. Horrified at Luther's attack on the sacraments, Henry had written a learned defense of the Catholic teaching on the sacraments, which had earned for him the glorious title of "Defender of the Faith." Sensuality, however, was to ruin him.

Married to Queen Catherine, the daughter of Ferdinand and Isabella of Spain, Henry had been very unfaithful to her over the years. Despite this fact and the fact that their only child was a girl, Mary, Henry had no thought of trying to rid himself of Catherine until he met a clever beauty named Anne Boleyn. Unlike the others, Anne would be satisfied with nothing less than the queen's crown. Henry conceived such a passion for her that he began to try to find a way to have her on her own terms. But what about Queen Catherine?

Catherine had been married previously to Henry's brother Arthur, who had died as a young boy of fifteen. Using this fact as a pretext, Henry now declared that his conscience troubled him because he had been married to his brother's widow—eighteen years before! However, the Pope had granted a dispensation before the marriage, so this supposed doubt was meaningless.

Henry VIII let nothing and no one
stand in the way of his passion

Anne was clever, and kept the king's desire at fever pitch while still demanding the throne. But Pope Clement VII could not give Henry the permission he wanted to reject Catherine and marry Anne.

Unfortunately, there were some men in high Church positions who were more politicians than anything else and were all too ready to find arguments to support the King, for their own advantage. Chief among them were Cardinal Wolsey, a thoroughly worldly-minded man, Thomas Cranmer, an evil-living priest, and Thomas Cromwell, an unscrupulous schemer.

With one political measure after another, King Henry threatened and pressured the bishops to agree to his view on the marriage problem, and to break their allegiance to the Vicar of Christ. In 1533, he secretly married Anne. Cranmer made a pronouncement of divorce between Henry and Catherine and announced that Anne was the King's valid wife and his Queen. Naturally, the result of these acts was the excommunication of Henry by the Pope.

From "in" to "of"

To save face and authority, the King declared that he himself was the "one supreme head on earth of the Church of England." Instead of the Catholic Church *in* England, he intended to make it the "Church *of* England"—with himself at its head. All the money previously sent to Rome was now to come into the royal treasury. Later, monasteries and churches were robbed of their incomes. Henry thus enriched himself and his nobles, to whom he turned over many religious houses and their properties. In this manner he made it advantageous to them to side with him against the Church's true Head.

Yet as far as doctrinal matters were concerned, the English king considered himself a Catholic and would not listen to the German Protestants who appealed to him to accept Lutheranism. In fact, he executed Cromwell with the accusation that he had spread wrong ideas about the Eucharist.

Execution was becoming very common in England now. Pride and sensuality completely ruled the king. He soon tired of Anne once he had her; moreover, the child she bore him was another daughter, not the male heir he ardently desired. Three years after she had been triumphantly crowned, he accused her of adultery and had her beheaded. Four more wives suffered at the hands of Henry! Ironically, two of them were named Catherine, like his first wife. Of these two, one was beheaded, and the other, his last wife, escaped death because he died first. Abbots and priests were put to death for refusing to accept him as head of the Church or for protesting his theft of all the monasteries in England; Protestants were also executed for denying the Real Presence of Christ in the Eucharist, although men who supported other Protestant ideas were often given bishoprics. It was truly an era of confusion and bloodshed.

When devoutly religious people began to realize what was happening, particularly when they saw the religious houses being seized by the king, thousands revolted. In what they called a "Pilgrimage of Grace," thirty-five thousand peasants marched on London, determined to save the Faith in England. With promises and threats, Henry put down the revolt, and later executed the leaders.

What of the bishops? So great was the power and influence of the king, so absolute was the idea of monarchy he and his father had built up, that nearly all the bishops of England gave in to him. There was one famous exception, Bishop John Fisher. He and his great companion, Thomas More, were the most illustrious of the English martyrs.

Thomas More:
witty, holy, fearless

St. Thomas More is one of the most fascinating men history offers for our study. He was a lawyer whose great intelligence had come to the attention of Henry VIII and who had reluctantly become more and more favored with authority. At last the King exalted him to the position of chancellor.

More was a great *humanist*, which means that he was interested in noble thoughts, new ideas, in scholarship—he even educated his daughters, which was very unusual at that

A family man, a statesman, a saint

time!—and in everything that makes this life more beautiful. He kept a menagerie of imported animals to delight his many guests!

Witty, gentle, the well-known author of the book, *Utopia*, Thomas More was at the same time very close to God, a deeply spiritual man who loved to meditate on heaven and whose heart was detached from earthly fame and success.

Brilliant as he was, More knew how quickly Henry could change his mind. Thus, when his son-in-law spoke with awe of how highly the King thought of his chancellor, More wisely replied, "If my head stood in the way of a French castle the King wanted, it would not long remain on my shoulders!"

Not a French castle, but a cunning temptress named Anne Boleyn soon proved how well More had judged his cruel, sensual master. St. Thomas More chose death rather than betray his Faith. In prison for a year before the beheading, he meditated on the sufferings of his Divine Master, Christ, and not even his wife's pleading made him hesitate to defend the primacy of Peter's successor as Vicar of Christ and Head of the Church.

To his beloved daughter, Margaret, he gave the tortuous hair shirt he had for years worn as a penance, unknown to any of his family or friends. He asked her to dispose of it secretly; no showy piety was his. At the scaffold, he was his calm, kindly self, and even joked, removing his beard from the block with the quip that *it* was not guilty of treason! And so died this marvelous man, who, almost single-handedly, against cowardly bishops and greedy courtiers, had witnessed to the indivisibility of the Church.

Bishop John Fisher of Rochester had been beheaded just two weeks before, at the age of eighty. He had been a zealous reformer, seeking to renew the Church, and setting the example himself by living a holy life. He was, in fact, so revered by the people that Henry had been afraid to take action against him when Bishop Fisher defended Queen Catherine's rights. But when he refused to swear allegiance to the king as head of the church, his fate was sealed. In a rage, Henry decreed his death.

St. John Fisher dressed for his execution with all the gaiety and care of a man on his way to a wedding. As he laid his head on the block, he murmured confidently, "In You, O Lord, I have hoped."

Edward, Mary, and Elizabeth

On the death of Henry VIII, his nine-year-old son, Edward VI, born of his third marriage, became king and head of the church. A council of nobles, however, was to rule until Edward grew of age. Edward died of tuberculosis six years later at the age of fifteen. In those six short years, Lutheran and Calvinistic practices and beliefs were introduced and enforced, especially by Cranmer. Bishops who objected were imprisoned.

At Edward's death, his half-sister, Mary Tudor, became Queen. She was the Catholic daughter of Catherine of Spain, Henry's first wife. Mary restored England to the Catholic Church, for her faith was deep and strong.

"I would far rather lose ten crowns than put my soul in danger," she declared. But Mary's methods were not always the wisest, and though she had great courage, she lacked personal charm and graciousness in dealing with people. Moreover, she married Philip of Spain, a marriage which the English resented because they were afraid that their country's independence would be lost to the foreign influence. Their national pride and honor was hurt. Thus, although the country as a whole joyously welcomed the return to the faith, there was still some doubt and discontent, and it grew when Queen Mary put to death those who had previously promoted the break with the Church. Many of them, if not all, had been in the various revolts aimed at driving Mary from the throne.

Queen Elizabeth I
of England

Mary Tudor died after reigning only five years. She was succeeded by her half-sister Elizabeth, Henry VIII's daughter by Anne Boleyn. Elizabeth's one aim was to please the majority of the powerful noblemen and encourage the nationalistic spirit in the people so as to ensure her popularity and her throne. She was gifted with uncommon intelligence and was very well educated. She was attractive, majestic in every sense, a lover of power and pageantry, and quick to sense what England wanted.

For such a woman, religion would never mean as much as her own power. She feared Catholicism because the Pope was a foreign power, but she liked its magnificent liturgical celebrations which she could not have in Calvinism.

For some time, she "felt her way," swinging between the "old religion," still practiced by most of the English, and the "new religion," which was gaining followers among the wealthier middle class. Finally, she built up the official Church of England, or Anglican Church, in which the ruler holds supreme authority, and which has a liturgy closely resembling the Catholic Mass, but differs in many doctrinal teachings. Anglicanism became so entwined with loyalty to the Queen and to England's newly emerging glory as a world power that by the time Elizabeth died, after reigning forty-five years, it was very solidly established.

Where once there had been a united Christianity, there was now Catholicism, Eastern Orthodoxy, and Protestantism in its various forms.

Especially important

▶ TO REFLECT ON:

Events on the international and national scene in our own times have proven that, just as in the sixteenth century, so now, too, new nations and minority groups within nations sometimes consider the Church as connected with the powers they are fighting. So, while rejecting those whom they feel have treated them unfairly, they often reject the Church, too. By the will of Christ, however, the Church is not meant to be connected with any one race or people to the exclusion of others. The Church is to be *universal*.

Do you do anything to hurt her image? Do you ever look down on members of other races or other neighborhoods, on those who are poorer or less popular? If so, since you are a

Catholic Christian, some may think that the Church has no place for them....

▶ TO STRIVE FOR:

Try to show in actions and manner that you know Christ expects you to radiate His love of others different from you — in any way. Be an instrument of peace, as St. Francis of Assisi prayed to be, sowing love where there is hatred. Try to see things "through the other fellow's eyes" before you pass judgment. Check carefully any attitude of personal superiority, which is so un-Christian.

▶ TO TALK TO GOD ABOUT:

Unity and brotherhood, an end to hatred, prejudice and strife — these are the things we all want. The Church, the *community* of God's People, is meant to be the home of unity for all.

Pray:

Even under the human face of Your Church, O Jesus, we find *Your* divine face, we find You Yourself! You it is who live in the Church, You it is who rule it, guide and sustain it down through the centuries.

Lord Jesus, make us devoted faithful of Your Church!

Within Your Church, O Lord, we are all present and united. Never are we alone!

United with You, who unite us among ourselves, we pray the *Our Father.*

Lord Jesus, guide us all to the Father, within Your Church!

Make of all Christians one single body, within Your Church! (Pope Paul VI)

RENEWAL WITHIN AND A HARDENING OF THE WALLS

"We know from history that periods of extraordinary productiveness follow every council. The Holy Spirit breathes through them, raising up generous, heroic vocations. He gives the Church the men she needs, the right men."

John XXIII

"The mass of Christians keeps moving
   ahead.
There is a small, closely-knit nucleus.
   The rest follow behind in a haphazard way,
      doing the best they can—
      but they do follow."

A. DE BOVIS

The period of the Catholic counter-reformation shows the Church seriously, humbly righting the wrong practices that had marred her beauty as Christ's Mystical Body. The Council of Trent, under the guidance of the Holy Spirit, set forth Christian doctrine in exact terms, clearing up much confusion. Following its decrees, Popes, bishops and saints in every part of Europe lifted clergy and laity to new heights of real Christian living.

The missions form a glorious chapter of this period of re-invigorated faith, as newly discovered lands opened up new fields "ripe for the harvest."

On the darker side, the Moslems again threatened the existence of Christendom before they were finally defeated. And worse, walls of division hardened between Orthodox, Catholic and Protestant Christians. Indeed, the separation was embittered by oppression and bloody battles.

The Council of Trent

Many theologians in the Church had undertaken to reply to Luther from the start, but until the Popes and bishops themselves set to work to reform the evils crippling the Church, little could be accomplished. A general council was badly needed also, to present Catholic teaching clearly regarding the matters with which Protestants disagreed, for there was much confusion. So it was that the *Council of Trent* came into being.

Trent, which was held in three sessions over a period of eighteen years, did not only aim to "answer the Protestants." Indeed, in the beginning, there had been hope that the two groups could meet in council, but the attempt failed. Despite the love of Scripture and warm piety Catholics and Lutherans could share; despite the humble adoration of the Almighty and the insistence on good morals which Catholics and Calvinists could share; despite the rich liturgy and prayer life that Catholics and Anglicans could share, the fundamental difficulty was religious faith: the power of the Catholic Church to teach faith and morals without error, as our Lord had guaranteed to her, until the end of time.

Protestants viewed Catholics as refusing to reform evil practices, and each of the groups within Protestantism looked with distrust at the other. Catholics knew that though some practices and people within their Church needed reform, it still remained the true Church of Christ. Therefore, they could only consider Protestants as heretics separated from the true faith and hopelessly divided among themselves. Sincere men in all the groups often doubted the sincerity of the others....

Our separated brethren

Still, the council did not condemn by name any of the famous Protestants when it set forth the Catholic teaching on the way man is saved, on original sin, on the sacraments, especially the Eucharist, the Mass. It was evident that the bishops of the council wanted to leave open the possibility of future dialogue with those whom St. Peter Canisius was to begin to call *"our separated brethren."*

On all the burning issues of the day, the Council of Trent spoke clearly. It upheld all *seven* sacraments, explained the effects of each one, stressed that marriage cannot be broken by divorce, set forth the true doctrine on indulgences, on devotion to the saints, and so forth. Thus, most of the confusion within the Church disappeared after Trent. A general council of Pope and bishops cannot err when setting forth doctrines of faith and morals.

In the matter of reform, a great step ahead was taken with the institution of *seminaries*. The problem of ignorant, worldly priests would be solved by educating and forming future priests in special schools called seminaries. Here, over a long period of years, their character would be formed, their minds instructed, and their spirituality deeply rooted. Unsuitable candidates would be dropped. Thus, from a worthy clergy, the Church could draw her bishops, cardinals and Popes. Once her ministers were good, her people could be led along the paths of holiness.

Philip Neri, a beloved figure in the streets of Rome

Philip Neri, God's comedian

The new system of seminaries and the betterment of priestly candidates were especially promoted by St. Francis de Sales; Jean Jacques Olier, who founded the Sulpicians, an order expressly dedicated to priestly training; St. John Eudes, St. Vincent de Paul, and St. Philip Neri.

Philip Neri spent his long life helping to uplift the spiritual life of clergy and laity in Rome. His was an odd spirituality, utterly different from the more famous founder of the Jesuits. Indeed, his congregation of the Oratory was originally just a group of his friends who got together to pray and talk of truth in a very simple, happy, informal manner. Friendliness and a wonderful brotherly love marked them.

Philip himself was always joking, playing pranks, making fun of himself in public — as when he went through the streets with his face shaved on only one side! His good humor was contagious, but no one who came to know him was fooled for long by his jokes: it was his way of covering up his great holiness, his tremendous works of compassion and charity, his power to prophesy, to read men's minds, to obtain stupendous conversions!

For Philip and his great number of followers, Christian holiness and gaiety went hand in hand!

An age of "greats"

The whole period of new life in the Church is called the *Catholic Reformation.* It produced some very different and very splendid saints: a Pope, St. Pius V; two Carmelite reformers: St. Teresa of Avila and St. John of the Cross; four great Jesuits: the founder, Ignatius Loyola, the former Duke, Francis Borgia, the incomparable missionary, Francis Xavier, and the apostle to Germany, Peter Canisius; a reforming Cardinal appointed by his uncle the Pope, but not like most of these "family appointments": Charles Borromeo, who made Milan a model diocese; the apostle of Rome itself: the unusual Philip Neri; founders of new religious orders: Cajetan of Thiene and his Theatines, St. Anthony Mary Zacharia and his Barnabites, St. Jerome Emiliani and the Somaschi; St. Angela Merici and her Ursuline Sisters; St. Francis de Sales and St. Jane Frances de Chantal, founders of the Visitation nuns; St. Vincent de Paul and St. Louise de Marillac, founders of the Vincentians and the Daughters of Charity; and many, many more. It was a golden age in many ways.

Ignatius of Loyola, God's soldier

Everywhere religious orders were returning to their original fervor and holiness of life, while new orders were springing up. The greatest of these new societies was undoubtedly the Society of Jesus, founded by the soldier-saint, Iñigo de Loyola, better known as St. Ignatius Loyola. He was from the Basque region of Spain and spent the first part of his life as a cavalier, a noble soldier, who dreamed of heroic deeds, such as rescuing the Princess Catalina from the clutches of her insane mother, Queen Joanna. But at the battle of Pamplona, a cannon ball shattered his leg and cut short his career.

A new kind of romance started for Inigo

Alone with his pain and his thoughts, Iñigo began to read books quite different from the chivalric romances he had fed his dreams on. The Life of Christ and the lives of His saints led him to dream of being a knight of our Lord and His Blessed Mother. He felt a burning desire to "perform those great feats which the saints have accomplished for the glory of God."

Ad majorem Dei gloriam — "to the greater glory of God"! That was Ignatius' motto and the rallying slogan of his Society of religious priests and brothers, which he patterned after the lines of the army discipline he knew so well. The growth of the Jesuits took place with extraordinary speed.

One very remarkable thing about this new group was its unswerving obedience and service to the papacy. At a time when the Holy See had lost much of its prestige throughout Christendom, Ignatius of Loyola placed at the command of the Popes an army of strong, well-educated, generous men ready to go anywhere and to do anything asked of them by Christ through His Vicar, the Pope. Moreover, there would be no danger of ambition creeping in, for Jesuits were bound not only by the vows of poverty, chastity and obedience, but by the strict prohibition not to seek any high position in the Church. What great things they accomplished in Europe – especially through their marvelous educational system – and in the missions!

A study in personalities

Ignatius lived at the same time as Luther and Calvin. While Luther was in hiding at the Wartburg, translating the Bible and experiencing agonies of doubt over his spiritual problems and his new doctrine, Ignatius was at Loyola Castle recovering from his wound and trying to figure out how God wanted him to serve Him. It is interesting to contrast the characters of the three men who so dominated their age, Luther, Ignatius and Calvin. Ignatius did not have the violent, impetuous temperament of Luther, but he did share his combination of power and gentleness. He was calmer and kinder with others than the cold, unrelenting Calvin, yet resembled him in his ability to set down his religious ideals in clear, compelling language. Ignatius' *Spiritual Exercises* became extremely influential, and right down to this day, this book induces many to make a thoughtful, lasting commitment to the cause of Christ.

Like Luther and Calvin, Loyola had an incredible capacity for work. He drove himself mercilessly to accomplish what he felt the Lord expected from him. His Jesuits, with their vast network of excellent and very popular schools, were to train a new generation of fine Catholic priests and laity and provide the Church with capable intellectual defenders.

In perfect control of himself, Ignatius was the model of the kind of men he wanted for his society: healthy, intelligent, calm, prudent men, joyous and generous. No wonder that the Society of Jesus played such a major part in the glorious revival within Christianity!

The far-flung missions

The name "wars of religion" has been given to the many struggles that tormented Europe during the last half of the sixteenth century and the first half of the seventeenth. In France, the wars centered around the struggle with Calvinism. In the Netherlands, the problem was the desire to be free of Spanish control and to set up the Calvinist religion. The Thirty Years' War, in the Empire, was both religious and political, and once it was over, there was no more hope of regaining territories lost to Protestant rulers. In the British Isles, the Catholics were persecuted and in Scotland and England, only a small number remained. Ireland, though crushed and punished in every way, clung to the Catholic faith. It was an era of bloodshed and suffering.

**California's unforgettable
Junipero Serra**

Yet this situation at home did not prevent enthusiastic missionary activity during this very period. In fact, it is known in Church history as the greatest missionary era after the first preaching of the Gospel in the infant years of Christianity. In all fairness, it must be said that the Church had never ceased being a missionary Church, even during her "blackest" moments. Alexander VI himself, unworthy as he was in his personal life, had added support of the missions to other praiseworthy and well-planned undertakings.

It was, however, the thrilling discoveries being made in the New World that brought on the great missionary fervor of the sixteenth and seventeenth centuries. We remember the joy of Spain's Queen Isabella at the thought that Columbus' new lands could be ripe harvests for missionaries.

The drama in the New World

In North and South America, the Spanish and Portuguese missionaries, who were generally members of religious orders, accompanied the explorers, government officers and colonists. The old Indian culture was overthrown by the conquerors and thus while the new civilization took over, its religion did, too. Fortunately, on the whole, the missionaries to the New World were men of great goodness and zeal, who planted the faith solidly in the hearts of their new converts and who often protected them against disease and harsh treatment by the less noble of the European adventurers and conquerors. Indeed, the missionaries often risked punishment for protesting against the way some of the natives were enslaved.

St. Peter Claver, the Jesuit missionary, labored heroically, against all odds, at Cartagena, Colombia, for the Negroes who were victims of the abominable slave trade. Another apostle of Colombia was the Dominican St. Louis Bertrand. In Argentina, the appealing, warm-hearted Franciscan, St. Francis of Solano, won men to Christ with extraordinary success. The Dominican, Bartholomew de las Casas, fought bravely against the greediness and cruelty practiced by his fellow whites against the Indians of Central and South America. In the Southwest of the United States and all through California, Franciscans like the great Junipero Serra, planted one mission after another, as the names of modern cities testify: San Francisco, Santa Barbara, San Diego, Los Angeles, Santa Monica, San Antonio and many others.

Saints were not lacking among the peoples of the New World themselves: there were St. Rose of Lima, Peru, and St. Martin de Porres, also of Lima, the black son of a Spanish cavalier and a Negro dancer. Moreover, in Mexico, the Blessed Mother of God herself appeared, with Indian features and skin color to a simple native, Juan Diego, to show God's love and mercy toward the humble, oppressed natives. *Our Lady of Guadalupe* became the beloved Patroness of the New World.

The American Indians

The French also sent missionaries to North America, following their own explorers and government officials. But it should be noted that it was the French colonists themselves who made up the Catholic community of Canada, just as the English Protestants were colonizing the territory southwards, which was to become the United States. There were few marriages between the whites and the Indians, as had taken place in Central and South America, where the faith thus took root among the original inhabitants.

Efforts were made, of course, to bring the Gospel to the Indians. The Jesuits known today as the North American martyrs are heroic proof of these efforts, and the saintly Indian maid, Kateri Tekawitha, is a marvelous flower thereof. Moreover, another Jesuit, Father Peter de Smet, working out of St. Louis, met with considerable success with American Indians.

In the English-speaking colonies, the struggle between the white men and the Indians was so bitter as to prevent any great union.

Moreover, since the number of Catholics settling in the United States was low in comparison to the Protestant colonists, government policy toward the Indians, once their power had been broken, was to assign them Protestant ministers, even if they had been evangelized by the "Blackrobes," as the Indians called the Jesuit missionaries.

St. Francis Xavier in the Far East

Sixty-two thousand miles he traveled in a ten-year period, the greatest missionary after St. Paul the Apostle! His name?

Only death stopped St. Francis Xavier

Francis Xavier, the handsome Spanish nobleman who was so dear to the heart of Ignatius Loyola. At the age of thirty-five, he left the beloved Founder, never to see him again, and set off for India. India, Malacca, Malaysia and Japan heard him preach Christ Crucified—and still he thirsted for greater conquests in the name of Christ. After returning to organize matters in Goa, India, he set out again over the dangerous seas, facing the threat of pirates and disease, as he had done so many times before. But now his face was set for China, the great, mysterious land he hoped to penetrate.

God willed otherwise. On a lonely island, just outside the gateway to China, this gallant missionary died of a burning fever. He had been a pioneer, and although many of his converts throughout the vast Buddist-dominated lands would fall away, still the seed had been planted. The secret of his unconquerable spirit which had driven his agonized body on, right to the door of China, was his union with Christ. So overwhelming was the love the Lord frequently showed him that sometimes he was compelled to murmur: "Enough, dear Lord, enough! I cannot take any more!"

What a son of Loyola was the once proud, ambitious lord of Xavier!

Japan's secret Catholics

The Church in Japan enjoyed a wonderful growth until a combination of events brought on persecution. The first persecution was on a small scale, but it gave the Church the *twenty-six Martyrs of Nagasaki:* Franciscan priests, Jesuit lay-brothers, young and old men, and even three children were crucified on February 5, 1597. Their marvelous constancy and joy in the face of execution, and particularly the courage of the children, who comforted grieving relatives, served to increase admiration for Christianity. By 1612, approximately 500,000 Japanese had become Christians.

In 1614, the ruler, Shogun Ieyasu banished all missionaries and had Catholic churches destroyed. Only a handful of priests remained, ministering in secret. Japanese Catholics, especially under Shogun Yemitsu, were tortured in every way imaginable, and without priests, the community could not survive. The amazing thing is that quite a number of them managed to hold to the faith secretly, teaching it to their children, and passing it down from one generation to the next.

Their discovery came in the nineteenth century when Catholic priests were finally allowed to go to Japan to serve the French Embassy.

One day, a few representatives of these secret Catholics called on them to ask them three questions: "Do you believe in the Mother of God? Are you unmarried? Do you follow the

The martyrs of Nagasaki

great Father in Rome?" When they replied "yes" to all three questions, they were satisfied that they were truly priests, and they revealed their faith — to the utter amazement and joy of the missionaries! The world outside had thought Christianity was utterly dead in Japan!

China

The ancient Empire of China was the object of great longing on the part of Francis Xavier, who died on December 3, 1552, just outside its gate, and of many another fervent missionary soul. The man who was to open the great land to Christ about a half a century later was an Italian Jesuit, Matteo Ricci. A talented painter, a learned, gracious person, he developed a missionary tactic which was to prove very successful.

**Emperor San-li was intrigued
with Father Ricci's maps**

Father Ricci learned the Chinese language, religions, philosophies, literary masterpieces, and customs. He then began to associate with the scholars of the country and to explain to them and even to the Emperor San-li the scientific instruments he had brought from the West. He dressed as a Chinese mandarin, used the Chinese version of his name, and never omitted any of the customary ceremonies which were so much a part of Chinese courtesy. As a result, he was given wonderful opportunites to preach freely. From his knowledge and understanding of their philosophies and literature, he could explain the teaching of Christ in a way that made it clear and appealing to them. It did not seem the "religion of foreigners." Thus, when he died, about 2,500 of the Empire's upper class were Christians. Forty years later, as Father Ricci had hoped, through these influential men, working with more Jesuits who followed in his footsteps, there were about 150,000 Catholics in China.

The Philippines, Java, Persia, India—what labors were expanded throughout these mission lands by Jesuits, Dominicans, Franciscans, Carmelites. It was certainly the "age of the missions."

Don Juan at Lepanto

When Pope Paul III ascended the papal throne in 1534, he found, as he later declared to the Council of Trent, "the Turks advancing on land and sea; Rhodes lost; Hungary devastated, Italy, Austria and Slavonia threatened." Once again, the Moslem threat was a very real one. Solyman the Magnificent was a very ambitious, capable sultan.

Christendom's hopes mounted, however, when his son, Selvin, assumed power, for Selvin was in no way his father's equal. Pope St. Pius V sent appeals to the Christian courts of Europe for another crusade to deliver Christendom from the threat. The response was excellent, and on October 7, 1571, while the Pope had the Rosary recited publicly, the great sea-battle of Lepanto raged. Don Juan of Austria, a young man of twenty-four, was in command of the huge fleet recruited from all over Europe.

It was a thrilling battle, hard-fought and furious. At the end of the day, which a grateful Pope was to consecrate in honor of Mary, Queen of the Holy Rosary, the Christians were completely victorious! The hymn, Te Deum, echoed across the Gulf of Lepanto from grateful hearts.

"There was a man sent from God, whose name was John!" cried St. Pius V, when the news of Don Juan's success reached Rome.

"I came, I saw, God conquered!"

But by the following century, the Turks were again a menace to Christian Europe. The Grand Vizier Köprili reorganized the Empire of the Ottoman Turks, and with his thousands of Tartars, attacked the West once more. The slave markets of Constantinople were doing a great business in Christian slaves!

The papacy again assumed the responsibility of calling another crusade and an international army came into being. Near St. Gothard monastery on the island of Roab, these forces, joined by six-thousand young French nobles who fought gloriously, stopped a Turkish army of 200,000.

But the Moslems struck again and again. The decisive battle was at Vienna in 1683. The Catholic rulers of Europe had again responded to the appeal of Pope Innocent XI. Students and ordinary townspeople defended their city side by side with the imperial troops. But the Turkish army numbered 250,000, and it was not until King John Sobieski of Poland led his 25,000 men in a gallant charge that the tide of victory turned.

"I came, I saw, *God* conquered!" declared the devout, humble Sobieski, paraphrasing Caesar's proud cry after crossing the Rubicon: "I came, I saw, I conquered!"

In the years that followed, the armies of the Moslem Crescent were driven out of Hungary. Then the war was carried right into the Ottoman Turkish Empire. By 1718, Turkish power had been completely broken in the whole Balkan area.

Moscow — a third Rome?

We have already seen how Christian unity was torn apart by the Catholic-Protestant strife. Now we look to the East and find that the Turkish conquests continued to help prevent any communication between Eastern Orthodox Christians and Catholics. Constantinople had gradually become the sole authority among the Orthodox, since the Moslems had permitted the Constantinople patriarch to precede the other once-important Church centers at Alexandria and Antioch. However, within Eastern Christianity, there were many small groups which refused to submit to the religious authorities at Constantinople. Thus, disunity was the picture within the Orthodox area, too.

Still, another Christian center was to appear: Moscow. In the fourteenth century, Moscow had induced the Patriarch of Russia to set up his residence there, and by the next century, she had become a famous capitol, both politically and religiously. The cunning tyrant, Ivan III the Great, had married a niece of Michael Palaeologus, the last Greek emperor, who died fighting on the walls of Constantinople. Now he declared that he was the true Byzantine emperor and the head of Orthodox Christianity, too.

"Moscow is a third Rome," said his theologians, "and there will never be a fourth." The Czar was supreme head of state and church, and he united his people to himself in hatred both of the Latin Christians and of the unbelieving Turks.

Ivan IV the Terrible developed the doctrine even further. An immoral man, much given to drink, to sensuality and cruelty, he nevertheless knew Sacred Scripture very well and liked to talk theology. Moreover, he often rose above himself to rule wisely and extend his Empire in all directions.

Completely dominated by the Czars, the Russian Church was soon faced with problems we have seen before in the West: drunkenness, ignorance, immorality among both the clergy and the people. The Patriarchs could do nothing, because they were at the mercy of the Czar. However, here, too, God raised up saints like Nil Sorski, who practiced great penance and preached against the worldly lives of religious, and Philip Solwotzk, whose life was an example of the compassionate charity of Christ.

Protestant and Catholic sufferings

The sixteenth and seventeenth centuries brought unbelievable suffering to countless numbers of good, sincere people in the name of religion. So much violence, so much bloodshed, so much injustice reigned in the name of faith! Protestants and Catholics alike were guilty of many, many mistakes and regrettable acts against one another in the latter half of the sixteenth century and in the seventeenth. Thus, despite the heroic efforts of noble-minded men on both sides, these two groups of Christians hardened in their opposition and mutual distrust.

By this time, Protestantism had become a way of life for many. They had been born into Protestantism and were proud of its traditions, its men and women who had gone to death for their beliefs, its hymns and services, the music it had brought forth, its literature, its many clean-living, hard-working believers. Yet many Catholics looked upon all of them as personally guilty of betraying the true faith.

On the other hand, Protestants often refused to recognize the elements of their faith that they owed the mother Church. They persisted in branding all Catholics as buried in error and darkness, as enemies to be despised.

Violence flared up over religion

Religion linked to power

Then, too, politics played a major part in the persecutions of both Protestants and Catholics. Rulers looked at religion, in many cases, with an eye to using it to strengthen their power over the people. And often, even when a ruler or nobleman was sincerely desirous of promoting his religion, he had other motives which were not so holy.

The mighty Spanish emperor, Philip II, for example, used the Inquisition — in fact controlled it — to rid the land of heretics, but as in other enterprises of this emperor it seems that his own interests were also very much in his mind. He apparently felt that by promoting the glory of Catholic Spain he was promoting God's glory. He prayed long hours, fasted, read St. Teresa of Avila's writings, and had a burning desire to reach sanctity. Yet where were the mercy and compassion for one's enemies that have always marked the saints? The Inquisition's victims did not see it.

Still, very little blood was shed in Spain in comparison to France and England.

Bloodshed in France

France was an especially pitiful sight in the second half of the sixteenth century and in the seventeenth. Though the faith was strong in the people, both Catholics and Protestants, they seemed to forget all human decency when they fought one another. Both groups massacred men, women and children and killed the wounded when they captured a city. Inhuman was their conduct — and all in the name of Christ! That was the horror of it.

One after another, the kings of France struggled with the problem of these bloody civil wars, the intrigue, the assassinations, and often they themselves contributed to the tragic situation. Henry III, a Catholic, was murdered, after having a Catholic rival murdered, and after joining forces with the Protestant Huguenots. The next king, Henry IV, was a Huguenot, but since the country was still mostly Catholic, this changeable man became a Catholic. He managed in four years to unite the country under him and make a peace treaty with Spain. It was during his reign that the *Edict of Nantes* was promulgated, April 13, 1598.

The Edict of Nantes is very important because it allowed a considerable number of religious liberties to the Huguenots, whereas other governments were forcing the ruler's religion upon the people. This edict has made Henry IV famous, for freedom of conscience was not the well-known and popular doctrine it is today. But we must be realistic and admit that the reason for the edict was mostly a practical one: it was a common-sense arrangement to stop the bloodshed. Devoted believers in both religions accepted it for that reason, and many accepted it out of sheer indifference to religion.

Louis XIV, the "Sun King," called Louis le Grand, revoked this Edict of Nantes, after he thought he had wiped out Protestantism. Indeed, in every country, the religious problem, when solved by wars or treaties, could always explode again in persecution and civil wars on the coming of a new ruler.

Louis XIV reigned over France from 1661 to 1715 in the days of her greatest glory. She was to become famous the world over as a powerful Catholic nation, a leader in culture and magnificence. In the decades preceding his reign, that is, the first half of the seventeenth century, new spiritual fervor had come surging forth. The majority of bishops were excellent men, faithful to the teachings of the Council of Trent. The priesthood took longer to uplift, but when the seminary plan began to function, it produced holy men of God. In fact, in this period, holy souls abounded in France: twenty-seven have been canonized by the Church!

The Sun King

Louis XIV was called the "Most Christian King," but his personal morals were decidedly "unchristian" during the first half of his life. Moreover, he seemed completely indifferent to the misery of the peasants of his land. He ruled with an iron will, but in his day, this absolute monarchy was common in Europe, and people and rulers alike felt that the king reigned by divine right.

The mighty monarch
being reproved in public

Majestic, awe-inspiring, the Sun King appeared devout, but not deeply so. Still, he admitted his sins remorsefully and was humble enough to allow great preachers to condemn his sins publicly in his very presence. Moreover, he stayed away from Communion rather than commit sacrilege, even though he knew people would talk. Always, even in his worst periods, he insisted on respect for the faith, for the laws of God. And in his later years, he seems to have undergone a real conversion.

Still, Louis XIV interfered too much in the affairs of the Church, and controlled all appointments to bishoprics and abbeys, thus reviving the evil practice that the reformers had stopped. He discouraged loyalty to the Holy See at Rome, which was to bring on a great many evils. At the same time, this very king strove to rid his land of all heresies. When he revoked the Edict of Nantes and began persecuting Protestants, thousands of them fled from France, amid much suffering. Those who remained and would not give up their belief began resisting with violence. Bloodshed came back to France.

Two other religious problems faced Catholicism in this country: two heresies.

Jansenism and Mérè Angelique

The Jansenist quarrel was the most serious of the two. Cornelius Jansen was a theologian of Louvain who felt that Calvinism had some Augustinian points on grace which should be accepted by the Church. At least, he *hoped* to have his doctrines accepted, since he did not want to break with the Church. The nuns at the convent of Port-Royal-des-Champs and Port-Royal in Paris supported this doctrine and its followers, even though the Church repeatedly condemned its heretical teachings.

"As pure as angels and as proud as devils" was the way Mérè Angelique Arnauld and her nuns of Port-Royal were described. Because of the king's interference in Church affairs, Mérè Angelique's influential father had obtained her position as abbess of the monastery when she was only eleven years old! And the little girl thought she would never be able to stand it. But in her teens a change came over her. She began to long to become a saint, to love Christ, and she started to reform herself and her community.

By the time she was twenty, this amazing girl had brought two large convents of nuns back to a strict, penitential life of real love of God and neighbor. Moreover, a number of other members of her family gave up wealth for a life of close union with God through prayer and penance.

How did this deeply religious woman, her nuns and her family end by being condemned by the Church they had thought to serve so well? Unfortunately, they were captivated by some eloquent preachers of Jansenist doctrines and especially by the gloomy, severe Jansenist way of life. Joy and confidence in God were frowned on; Holy Communion was to be received only very, very rarely by the nuns of Port-Royal and only after severe penances. After reading the Jansenists, no one would ever dare to think himself worthy to receive Holy Communion, declared St. Vincent de Paul.

When they were opposed, the Jansenist preachers and nuns refused to submit, refused to admit that their doctrine had any errors in it. In their proud zeal, they maintained that they alone were true Christians.

French Jansenism lasted right down to the nineteenth century, in one form or another, though often secretly. Its danger and its persistent popularity lay in the fact that it looked "so holy." For this reason, Rome, the king, nearly all the bishops, the Jesuits and the new, fervent seminaries all opposed it.

Quietism

Quietism was the second and less dangerous heresy. Taught by a priest named Molinos and spread in France by an excitable, rather unstable widow, Madame Guyon, Quietism was a false mysticism. It taught that one should do nothing at all to grow spiritually — make no effort, but just let God do everything.... This false doctrine encourages an all-too-easy spiritual life, a kind of spiritual laziness. "Trust God as though everything depended on Him, and work as though everything depended on you" has always been the Church's wise admonition.

When condemned, *Quietism* died out at once and completely. Fenelon, an eloquent and brilliant preacher who had accepted it in part, submitted humbly when Rome condemned his book.

The great danger of *Jansenism* lay in its spirit of rebellion against the authority of the Holy Father, as established by Christ, and in its refusal to let its followers be nourished frequently by Christ in the Holy Eucharist. The "bread of heaven" was not meant to be a reward for men who consider themselves holy and worthy of it; it is the support and strength of us weak humans who sincerely want to better our lives and and our loyalty to our Lord.

The international situation

What of the papacy during the sixteenth and seventeenth centuries? Its "dark period" was long past. St. Pius V had died in 1572, after striving mightily to carry out the healthy reforms of the great Council of Trent. The Popes who followed him were not outstanding men, but they did their duty vigorously and zealously, and continued to purify and elevate the Church. By the opening of the seventeenth century, the Holy See enjoyed well-merited esteem at home and abroad.

As time went on, however, the respect for the Pope became restricted to spiritual matters alone. No longer was the Vicar of Christ also to be a powerful figure in political affairs. Though they often strove long and hard to promote peace between warring Christian nations, the Popes' appeals were frequently ignored. Powerful leaders often made decisions affecting Christendom without even consulting the papacy.

Germany

Throughout Europe, the rulers were determined to keep religion, be it Protestant or Catholic, closely allied to their own individual thrones. In Germany, the situation was most confusing and dangerous. Different regions professed different religions according to the desires of their princes. Often, a Protestant prince persecuted not only the Catholics but also the Protestants of other sects. The same was true of Switzerland.

The Low Countries

In the Low Countries, a division was effected for religious reasons. The Northern Provinces became Protestant, as Holland has officially remained down to modern times. The Southern Provinces, which correspond approximately to modern Belgium, remained Catholic. In the early part of the seventeenth century, Dutch Catholics were allowed some freedom, but after 1648, persecution began and Masses had to be celebrated in secret.

Edmund Campion,
English Jesuit and martyr

England

In England, under Elizabeth, Catholics received brutal treatment. They were punished by death for giving shelter to priests; they were fined so heavily that utter poverty became their lot. From 1570 on, to do "anything Catholic" was considered high treason against the queen and the country. Priests from Europe were hunted down and put to death. The most famous of these martyrs is Edmund Campion, a handsome young Jesuit whose great love of his England (at his martyrdom he still prayed for Queen Elizabeth!) made him give up his life in the effort to keep the faith alive in the land. The martyred priests numbered one hundred forty-seven!

James I of Scotland was Elizabeth's successor, and under him, more anti-Catholic measures followed. Under the next king, Charles I, through the efforts of his Catholic wife, Henrietta of France, the restoration of the faith seemed a possibility, but Charles was reluctant to give up his supreme control over the Church. Then, too, he had to face a civil war, which he lost to the Puritans, who were strong Calvinists.

The Puritan Protector, Oliver Cromwell, granted liberty of conscience, but made it plain that this freedom was only for the Protestant Evangelical sects. He was bitter against Anglicans and had no mercy at all for Catholics.

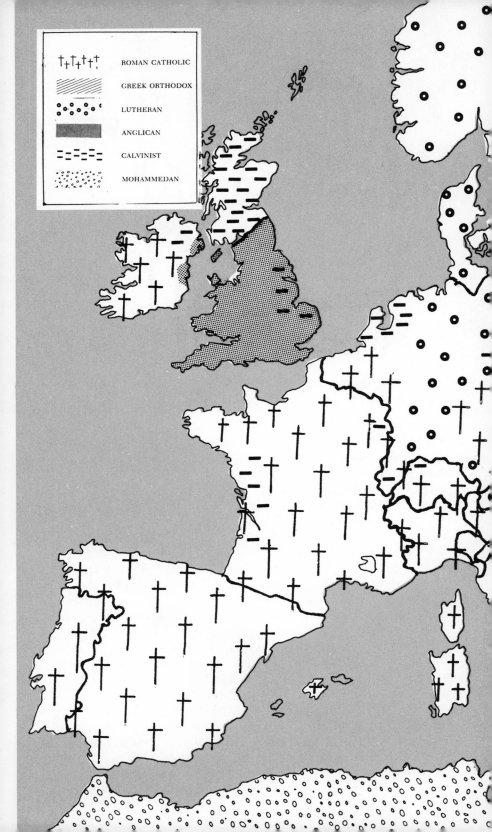

ROMAN CATHOLIC

GREEK ORTHODOX

LUTHERAN

ANGLICAN

CALVINIST

MOHAMMEDAN

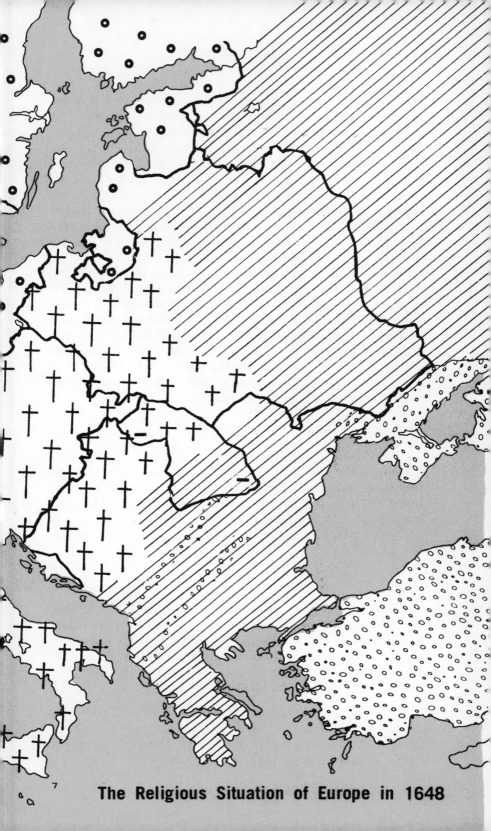

The Religious Situation of Europe in 1648

Ireland

Ireland was subjected by Elizabeth to a reign of terror, of bloody massacre. It was accompanied by wholesale repression of every freedom. Every attempt to revolt against this cruel slavery of an entire nation brought worse persecution. Yet all this only served to strengthen the Irish determination to cling to the Catholic faith at all costs. At the time that Cromwell was attacking King Charles I and the Royalists, the Irish patriots took advantage of the situation to revolt. In their anger, they turned on Protestants and massacred some. But the right to practice their religion, which Charles granted them in 1646, did not last long.

With savage zeal, Cromwell bore down on Catholic Ireland as soon as he was sure of his power. All the forces of resistance were put to death, deported, or banished to remote parts of the island. Most of the land properties belonging to Catholics were given to the English. Still the Irish held to their faith, spurned the Protestant ministers, risked their lives to hide priests, to hear Mass at the famous "Mass rocks" hidden in the woods. For centuries the Catholic faith burned brightly despite all the odds against it.

Bohemia, Hungary, Poland

In Bohemia and Hungary, Catholicism remained the religion of the land, and Protestants were persecuted, despite the pleas of various bishops on their behalf. In Poland, political upsets and rebellion brought on a crisis, and by 1655, Poland was in serious danger of losing her independence. As to their faith, the Poles and the Lithuanians remained staunchly Catholic.

Italy

Italy, too, though so divided politically, was ever loyal to the Catholic faith. The only heretics, called Waldensians, were few and a Duke of Savoy was guilty of a terrible slaughter of these people, even of their women and children.

Switzerland and Scandinavia

The same intolerance was evident in Calvin's Geneva, (Switzerland), where anyone who tried to convert to Catholicism was subject to the death penalty. However, several of the Swiss cantons and cities remained Catholic.

**Early pioneers in unity efforts
labored unsuccessfully**

In Scandinavia (Denmark, Norway and Sweden) severe laws wiped out Catholicism.

Scotland

In Scotland, where Knox's Calvinism was called Presbyterianism, the unhappy Mary Stuart tried in vain to restore Catholicism.

Married to the King of France, Francis II, she was left a widow while still a very young, very pretty girl. Back in her own country, she made a series of blunders, and was charged by her enemies with immorality and with being an accomplice in a murder. The charges have not been established. Her enemies revolted against her, but she managed to escape into England.

Elizabeth kept the Queen of Scots a prisoner for eighteen years. During this time, Mary grew very close to God through her prayers and sufferings.

At last, fearing that rebels might try to make Mary Queen of England, Elizabeth put her to death. After Mary, Presbyterianism reigned supreme in Scotland, and King James could succeed in establishing only a very small branch of Episcopalianism.

Early workers for unity

Walls of division stood strong everywhere in Europe. It was clear that force would never win converts, but yet kindness to members of other religions was very rare in these centuries. There were both Protestants and Catholics who urged men to work for unity, but for the most part they were unheeded. One of these, the famous Protestant, Hugo van Groot, or Grotius, was particularly distressed with all the divisions within Protestantism. He saw union with the Vicar of Christ as the only hope of Christian unity. Polish kings, an Italian Capuchin monk named Magni and many other Catholics also tried to bring about a reunion of Protestants and Catholics, but all these men suffered a great deal for their efforts and were unsuccessful.

Too much bitterness and violence had occurred for the majority of men to be ready to listen to one another and concentrate on what they had in common. Moreover, it cannot be denied that some differences were and are essential ones: the teaching power of the Pope and bishops, the seven sacraments, and the sacrifice of the Mass.

Monsieur Vincent and the Church of the poor

The situation of the lower classes, of the poor peasants, was one which cried out for mercy. Yet during all the wars, amid all the glitter and gold of palaces and mansions, few seemed vitally concerned over their misery.

Then came St. Vincent de Paul, better known as "Monsieur Vincent," a forerunner of many modern social apostles. This great man has to his credit the founding of a congregation of priests who went everywhere to preach missions and revive the faith; he himself, with his simple, straightforward sermons, and even more, with the example of his own life, converted many members of the nobility and even of royalty to truly Christian lives. Moreover, Monsieur Vincent helped give the Church dedicated, holy priests by the model seminaries he founded. All this he did, but he is best known for his magnificent works of charity.

It is as the Apostle of Charity that he is usually pictured: feeding and sheltering starving, destitute peasants, nursing the sick, organizing vast channels of relief, taking the place of a galley slave chained to the oars of a ship. And his own overflowing love proved contagious. Literally thousands of Frenchmen—and especially women—listened to his appeal on behalf of the poor.

The Ladies of Charity

Young, wealthy women found in works of charity a joy their parties and jewels had never given them. Somehow Vincent had a way of convincing them, and even Queen Anne, that their jewels would serve them better if sold for the poor.

**St. Vincent de Paul
set in motion a great wave of charity**

The "Ladies of Charity," as the new group of social apostles were called, taught the children of the poor, nursed in free hospitals, visited the needy to care for them. What an unforgettable picture of the love of Christ were these noble ladies ministering to their unfortunate brothers in the poorest, unhealthiest sections!

Another saint, the widow Louise de Marillac, joined St. Vincent, to become the co-foundress of the Daughters of Charity, a congregation of sisters. Like him, she had spent

the first part of her life absorbed in affairs of high society, but
had then come to give herself to God, heart and soul. St.
Louise was a strong-willed, humble, clear-thinking woman.
She and her spiritual daughters, the first sisters to devote
themselves to an active apostolate out among the people, supported Monsieur Vincent in all his works, in schools, in visits
to the poor, in prisons, in hospitals, in homes for orphans, for
juvenile delinquents, for beggars. There was no human misery that did not find a Christian response in the compassionate
hearts of Saints Vincent and Louise.

What wonderful representatives they were of the compassionate Church of the compassionate Christ, open to the
world's wounds, humbly, lovingly holding out the fraternal
hand of charity in an age so sorely in need of it.

Especially important

▶ TO REFLECT ON:

Immature people take scandal at the inevitable human
imperfections found in the Church, in the past and in the
present. Immature people also are tempted to argue violently
with those whose beliefs are different. Still others, when
faced with an argument they cannot answer, or an unworthy
action on the part of some Church figure, conclude that the
Church is wrong and turn away from her.

The mature follower of Christ acts quite differently. He
plunges deeper into the mystery of the Church, praying and
studying her better, thus turning his childhood faith into a
deeper, more mature belief. The sight of cowardice or other
forms of failure to love only serves to make him want to be
twice as committed to Christ.

▶ TO STRIVE FOR:

Look for chances to put your faith into action. Get into
things. Put some spark into the Church or school organizations
that everyone is criticizing as being dull. Where there is
criticism, put love and positive action. Don't be satisfied until
you realize that others see you as a person with an aim in life,
with a personal, well-thought-out commitment to Christ and
His Church, as one always ready to share that faith, that way
of life. And if you disappoint yourself, be patient with yourself. Let it be true of you, on a small scale, what G. K. Chester-
ton said of the Church:

"It is perfectly true that the ship sank;
but it is far more extraordinary that the
    ship came up again:
    repainted and glittering, with the cross
    still at the top.
This is the amazing thing the religion did:
it turned a sunken ship into a submarine."

► TO TALK TO GOD ABOUT:

Lord, I'm no Ignatius Loyola or Teresa of Avila
    or anybody big like that.
    I don't know much about self-sacrifice and
    contemplation, and my works of love
    and apostolate look pretty insignificant to me.
Lord, I know more about yard lines and movies and
    bowling alleys and money — well, You know —
    than I do about the bigger things.
But these things are big, real big to me now.
Still, I don't want to be swallowed up by events and
    things and gimmicks. Let me find You, Christ Jesus,
    in all this, and especially in the people who are
    coming to mean a lot to me.
When I talk, let something sensible come out. When I
    get hot, cool me off. Don't let me think I know every-
    thing and make the mistakes history shows have been
    made so many times already. Steer me clear of self-
    ishness — and let me keep growing in You.

7

A
TIME
OF
REVOLT

"Every age brings a new attack upon the faith."

H. de Lubac

"...The Christian religion, of all the religions that ever existed, is the most humane, the one most favorable to freedom and to the arts and sciences. The modern world is indebted to it for every improvement, from agriculture to the abstract sciences, from the hospitals for the unfortunate to the churches built by the Michelangelos and adorned by the Raphaels. Nothing is more divine than its morality, nothing more lovely and more sublime than its beliefs, its doctrine, and its worship. It encourages genius, corrects tastes, develops the virtuous passions, gives energy to ideas, presents noble images to writers, and perfect models to artists. There is no disgrace in being believers with Newton and Bossuet...."

VISCOUNT DE CHATEAUBRIAND
Genius of Christianity

The absorbing events and personalities of this period will be viewed under the following headings:

the rationalist attack on faith and the charge that the Church is an enemy of science and progress;

the growth of revivalism in Protestantism;

American religious history, and the spread of the Church in other mission lands;

the religious history of the Negro people;

the revolutionary movement in Europe and its effects on the Church;

the renewed position of the Papacy and an account of the First Vatican Council.

The battle of ideas

Someone has said that the greatest battles are fought not on the battlefields of the world, but in the minds of men. In following the fascinating growth of the Church and her progress through history, we have seen many political struggles and much strife over theological matters between Christians. Now, in the eighteenth century we find new thinkers, new philosophies lined up against faith, against Christ and His Church.

Listen, for example, to the hatred smouldering in the words of one of the Church's bitterest enemies: "I'm tired of hearing that twelve men were enough to establish Christianity. I yearn to prove that only one is needed to destroy it!" The man was Voltaire, and his slogan against the Church was *"Crush the infamous thing!"*

Voltaire was a *rationalist.* Although this alone would not have made him such a foe of Christianity, it is important to understand what Rationalism is and why a writer such as Voltaire could have been so popular and influential among a certain class of intellectuals in a Catholic country like France.

Rationalism is not an easy term to define, but we might say that it is an over-emphasis of the intellectual ability of man. Extreme rationalists exalt man's mind to the point where he accepts as true only what he can reason to — thus rejecting any knowledge that would come by God's revelation. So this movement led men to make a complete split between reason and faith.

The genius of St. Thomas Aquinas had also shown the marvelous achievements of which the human mind is capable, but he showed, too, that our faith opens our minds to even vaster fields of truth. In other words, reason and faith are meant to work together in perfect harmony. With rationalism, a division was introduced between the two.

The weapon of sarcasm

René Descartes, a seventeenth century philosopher, is called the father of Rationalism. All his life he aimed to be a devout Catholic and he never knowingly intended to set the human mind on the path of revolt against faith, which actually he did, however.

About one hundred years later, the separation of faith and reason had led to a denial of faith, because some philosophers wrongly concluded, first that faith was not important, and later, that it was *against* reason. *They could never prove this,* but it was their extreme emphasis on merely natural truths that led them to such a mistaken view of reality. They became blind to the sublime truths that lift the human mind to soaring heights.

Indifference to faith, joined to evil moral conduct, produced men who began to look on the Church as the enemy of reason — forgetting that it was this very Church that had saved Western civilization from becoming barbarian! It was this very Church which had founded the medieval universities, the homes of the true use of reason. It was this Church that was the foundress of a vast system of schools all over Europe!

It became "fashionable" in eighteenth century Europe for the superficially-educated, the so-called "intelligentsia," to write and read sarcastic books poking fun at Christian faith and morals. In elegant French *salons,* the new "philosophers" met to entertain each other with their jibes. They were almost childish in their efforts to outdo one another at this "game."

**Scientific studies
attracted universal interest**

Science was another almost magical word in the eighteenth century, and strangely enough, the scientific movement was used by some to support their attack on faith. Newton and his laws of motion, Franklin and electricity, Linnaeus and his classification of living things, Watts and his steam engine — this progress in man's conquest of his world thrilled everyone.

But while some glorified God all the more for the marvels He has put at man's disposal, others began to think that man, by himself and by his brains alone could do anything. Puffed up by senseless pride, they acted as though they no longer needed God. Naturally, deeper thinkers realized that although man is to be praised for discovering nature's tremendous secrets, God is far more to be praised for creating nature and its wonders in the first place!

Galileo

The foes of the Church sought to make her appear the enemy of progress, an obstacle in the path of science. Again and again they pointed to the famous *"Galileo affair"* as proof.

Galileo was a seventeenth-century scientist who built a powerful telescope and declared that he had scientific proof of the truth of the Copernican theory, that is, that the earth revolved around the sun. The common belief was that the sun revolved around the earth. Others before Galileo had held his theory, including the philosopher-Cardinal, Nicholas of Cusa. Moreover, the Popes had never spoken out against it. It was, in fact, the correct theory, as we know, even though Galileo's proofs were not sufficient. Galileo met with condemnation, however, because he moved into the field of biblical studies and seemed to be teaching that Sacred Scripture had errors in it.

Alarmed at this, a papal congregation supported the mistaken theory that the sun moves around the earth. The fact is that the Bible was never meant to be a manual of science, so the whole question should not have come up in the first place. Moreover, the mistake was no proof against the truthfulness of Christianity, since the Church is infallible in matters of faith and morals, not in scientific theories. But her attackers used this incident to brand her as an "enemy of progress."

Voltaire's hatred

François-Marie Voltaire was the most fanatic of the Church's enemies. He used his skill as a writer, a dramatist, and a poet to attack the clergy first, then Sacred Scripture, then the Church, and finally Christ our Lord.

His hatred seemed to have something desperate about it, as though he were actually afraid of the religion he was attacking. He was not like many an adversary, calmly hammering away at beliefs and good moral lives. No, Voltaire had to resort to passionate but false charges and coarse, indecent writing, even about so beloved a French heroine as St. Joan of Arc.

Together with Denis Diderot, Jean d'Alembert and others, he did much to turn men away from a joyous, optimistic faith and to blacken their lives with a bitter emptiness that no vulgar joke could brighten. It is no coincidence that just eleven years after the death of this man who charged the Church with all kinds of crimes, the French Revolution broke out, religion was attacked, and a bloody terror reigned such as had never been seen before.

In England and Germany, Protestantism, too, suffered serious blows from rationalistic freethinkers, just as Catholicism did in France.

Yet Voltaire and men like him only served to prove still another time that the Church is the work of God and cannot be wiped out.

New forms of Protestantism

Right from the start, it was clear that free interpretation of the Bible would lead to constant divisions. Each branch of Protestantism, as it established itself in a nation, desired to be *the* Church there and to prevent any differing beliefs from gaining ground. "Protestors" were, therefore, denied the right to protest, the right to private, personal interpretation of the Bible—the very right on which the first dissenters had insisted!

Despite these efforts, new Protestant groups kept appearing on the scene, and their founders were often as passionately dedicated to their beliefs as Luther and Calvin had been.

John Wesley, founder of the Methodists, is a good example. This pale, thin Englishman was one of the nineteen children born to his devout Anglican mother, who daily read the *Imitation of Christ,* a favorite Catholic book.

John wanted to live a life of prayer, fasting, meditation on the Bible, and charity to the poor. He began to gather disciples who would follow him in his total dedication to Christ.

As a good Anglican [Church of England] minister, he tried to make his movement a reform of that Church, but it turned into a new religion called *Methodism.*

Wesley's brother Charles wrote immensely popular hymns which helped promote the movement, and John's ardent preaching in the fields and squares won many followers, especially among the poor whom he loved and helped.

The Methodists were persecuted at first, but eventually tolerated. In the meantime, despite Wesley's intention, the revivalist character changed, and the new religion settled into a regular church pattern. Moreover, after his death, it split up into several groups. As a result, there are some twenty different branches.

It was John Wesley's praiseworthy insistence on brotherhood, based on deep faith, that was to contribute much to the "American dream" of a good life for all men.

Pietism and the Quakers

Another form of Protestantism which was to take root in American soil was *Quakerism.* Protestantism was suffering badly from the attacks of rationalists. The established Church of England, that is, the Anglican Church, the Lutheran Church in Germany, and other churches throughout Europe, were losing followers. Many people in these official churches no longer believed. They were Christians in name only.

Grieving over this situation, groups of Protestants in Germany, Sweden, and other countries banded together to live lives of piety and charity. The movement was called *Pietism;* it was a reaction against the established Protestant churches and against the unbelieving philosophers.

Pietism minimized dogmas and emphasized the effort to lead Christlike lives. It cultivated religious emotions and was frankly mystical.

Many Pietists claimed to have mystical experiences, ecstasies and special revelations from the Holy Spirit. The leaders deeply stirred their followers with love for the crucified, thorn-crowned Christ, and in one model city of pietists, the night silence was often broken by the beautiful chorale singing of hymns such as "Side of Christ pierced by a lance."

All this upsurge of piety was very important for Protestantism, which was so hard hit by the sneers and religious indifference of the "new" philosophers and thinkers. In Catholic countries, instead, while some intellectuals were led astray, the vast majority of the people held firmly to their faith.

The emotionalism of Protestant revivals and the emphasis on the heart rather than on the head often led to extremes. As one writer put it, there was a real "epidemic of ecstasy"!

The English Quakers were not exactly Pietists, but their founder, George Fox, believed strongly that the church should be a mystical, invisible church wherein the faithful would each receive interior light from God. This is the famous "illumination" doctrine of the Quakers, whose proper name is the Society of Friends. Living upright, honest lives, the Quakers showed love to one another, but, like the Puritans before them, drew angry resentment because of their plain, dark clothing and their loud protests against the established Protestant faiths. The movement never grew too strong, nor did two other similar sects, the Shakers and the "Jumpers."

Still other forms of Protestantism were the Baptists, the Anabaptists, the Mennonites, the Unitarians, the Brownists, etc. And within many of these churches, as within the Church of England itself, there were divisions and smaller groups or movements. Many of them came into being to get back to what their founders felt was a "pure" Christianity, without authorities or rules, and for many, even without the authority of the Bible. But as they grew, they always ended by setting up some kind of authority and creed, from which another generation of revivalists would then revolt....

Again and again, Protestant church history records these new revivals, or reform movements within its ranks, resulting in innumerable divisions, which it was powerless to stop, since there was no equivalent in Protestantism to the Vicar of Christ, the successor of Peter, whose authority is the rock of Catholic unity. Only in fairly recent times has a strong ecumenical or "unity" movement developed within Protestantism.

Christianity in Colonial America

Fervent reformed groups within Protestant England cast longing eyes on the new land of America, where they could be free to live their version of Christianity without being persecuted. Religion could begin anew, they thought, avoiding what they felt were the mistakes of Europe. Consequently, all the sects we have just mentioned transplanted themselves to the American colonies, as did the High and Low Churches of England and Scottish Presbyterianism, as well as other Protestant groups such as Lutherans and Calvinists from the continent of Europe.

The first English colony of Virginia, founded for trade purposes, became a bulwark of Anglicanism. The famous Plymouth settlement was the work of the Pilgrims, a division of the English Puritans. Persecuted, they had first fled to Holland and then to Plymouth in the New World. The Pilgrim Fathers form an important part of the American Protestant tradition.

The Massachusetts Bay colony was built by Governor John Winthrop along the lines of Calvin's city-church in Geneva. Low Church ministers and land-owners ruled the colony with sternness, from which many soon revolted. Roger Williams started a new colony at Providence, Rhode Island, where he allowed other Protestant sects freedom of worship.

Dutch Protestants started the prosperous colony of New Amsterdam, but the English claimed it as rightfully theirs in 1664, and took it by force, renaming it New York. Thus, in the New York Colony, the two principal religious bodies were the Dutch Calvinists and the Anglicans.

Two men of vision

Maryland and Pennsylvania have unusual religious histories. Sir Cecilius Calvert (Lord Baltimore) was a Catholic friend of King Charles I and Queen Henrietta Maria. In 1634, the King granted him a large piece of land above Virginia. Baltimore called it Maryland and opened it up to his persecuted English Catholic brethren, but he also threw it open to any and every Christian denomination. Maryland came to be the home of true American brotherhood, where Catholics, Puritans, Baptists and High Church Anglicans lived together peaceably.

When Puritans from Virginia gained control of Maryland, they persecuted Catholics and Anglicans alike. Eventually the Anglicans became supreme, but they continued the oppressive anti-Catholic laws.

The next tolerant community, Pennsylvania, was founded by William Penn. Pennsylvania means "Penn's Woods."

**Penn, the devout Quaker,
welcomed all Christians without exception**

Its capitol was at Philadelphia, which means "The City of Brotherly Love." Penn was a devout Quaker who had the faith and courage to build a colony which granted all Christians equal rights and which established friendly relations even with the Indians. People scoffed at his dream, but it came true, and Pennsylvania was a haven of peace, until William and Mary came to the throne of England.

Of all the British colonies, Pennsylvania was the only one that did not persecute Catholics. In this colony, Catholics could worship in the open.

Other colonies arose as a result of grants made by the kings. Georgia is especially noteworthy as having been born of the charity of a devout pietistic believer, General Oglethorpe. His dream was to make it a refuge for poor people who would otherwise be imprisoned in England for unpaid debts. The enterprise was not successful, because Oglethorpe imposed a very strict Methodist devotional life to which many did not care to submit.

In the South and West of what is now the United States, therefore, Catholic settlements were to be found, but along the Atlantic seaboard, the Thirteen Colonies preparing for the War of Independence in 1776 were all Protestant—divided in belief but united by pride in the faith of their staunch forefathers.

John Carroll, first U.S. bishop

A strange embassy set out for Canada just before the outbreak of the War of Independence in the Thirteen Colonies. It was composed of Benjamin Franklin, Samuel Chase and a priest named John Carroll. They were being sent by the colonial patriots to ask the Canadians to remain neutral and friendly toward the revolutionary forces in the coming war.

Who was this priest of whom the Protestant leaders thought so highly, despite the common antagonism toward Catholics? He was a Maryland-born priest who had studied in France and entered the Society of Jesus. Two years later, strong political enemies of the Jesuits succeeded in practically

**A staunch patriot
was the first U.S. bishop**

forcing the Pope to suppress the very Order that served him devotedly. Only in Russia did the Society of Jesus remain in existence, until it was re-established by another Pope forty-one years later.

Back in the colonies, Carroll joined other zealous priests in ministering to the small number of Catholics; there were only about twenty-five thousand in the whole colonial territory. When the war broke out, he urged the Catholics to throw themselves heart and soul into the fight. George Washington was so impressed by their patriotism that he wrote John Carroll personally, to tell him so.

When the great American Constitution was adopted, it contained the memorable words: *"Congress shall pass no law establishing any religion or prohibiting the free exercise of any religion."* The joy among long-persecuted groups, especially English-born Catholics, is not hard to imagine! Here, at last, they could breathe the air of freedom. No wonder that in the years ahead, tides of immigrants were to sweep onto American shores, a great number of them Catholics.

Pope Pius VI told the twenty-six priests in the American Colonies to choose from among their number the one they thought would be the best leader. John Carroll was their unanimous choice. He was first called the Prefect Apostolic, but five years later was made a bishop, with Baltimore as his diocese, the first in the United States. Just sixty years later, there would be about one million, six hundred thousand Catholics in the new nation! Guaranteed their rights by law, they still had to face tremendous social persecution. They were still a despised minority. Yet they remained firm and strong in their faith.

A saint of old New York

Typical of the fervor, love and vitality of the Church in the early days of the United States was *Elizabeth Bailey Seton.*

The beautiful daughter of a New York doctor, and a very devout Protestant, she married into the prosperous Seton family and lived an exemplary life as a Christian wife and mother. After her husband's death, the attractive young widow found herself drawn to the Catholic faith, especially to Christ in the Blessed Sacrament. Her decision to become a Catholic brought her great suffering, for her relatives and friends turned against her.

Alone with her children and very poor, she tried to open a little school, but ex-friends discouraged parents from sending their children to her. Still, Elizabeth rejoiced in these hardships as a chance to share in the sufferings of Christ. The steel-like spirit of this lovely woman was typical of youthful America — strong and sure in its convictions, unbending under pressure.

Beauty, faith and a great love marked Elizabeth Bailey Seton

Elizabeth Seton became the foundress of a new American community of sisters, modelled on the Daughters of Charity of St. Vincent de Paul. Her community of generous religious teachers became the Sisters of Charity of Emmitsburg, Maryland, the first of the hundreds of orders of sisters who would serve the Church in America.

The very *first* convent of American nuns, we should say, however, was that of the Carmelites of Port Tobacco, Maryland. It was made up of American Sisters who had joined the Carmelites in Belgium, and it was established in Maryland shortly after the American Revolution. Its descendant still flourishes in Baltimore.

Failures and successes

The eighteenth century witnessed many heroic missionary efforts, but taken as a whole, it was a very low period for the missions. Little headway was made in Africa for many

reasons: the hold of paganism, the conquests made by Mohammedanism, the vastness of the continent, the lack of knowledge about it, the scarcity of missionaries able to gain admit-
tance, and the terrible curse of the slave-trade.

In China, the paganism of the vast numbers of the people
and of the governments, and hatred for foreigners, succeeded
in almost wiping out the Christian missions. Disputes among
Christian missionaries helped the disasters along. For these
missionaries the problem was the ever difficult one of adaptation of Christian ideas to the customs and languages of
converts coming out of pagan cultures — such problems as the
word for God, or the honors paid to dead ancestors.

Chinese Christians remained steadfast under persecution; at length, a more glorious day dawned for them in the
nineteenth and twentieth centuries. Unfortunately, today
the Chinese Christians are suffering far worse persecution
from the Chinese Communists. But reports continue to come
through of the faithfulness of the great majority of them.

All the mission fields of the world suffered greatly when
the Jesuits were suppressed. Other generous priests tried to
fill the gap, but they were never enough.

"New France," however, is a bright spot in the picture.
The French missionaries and colonists who settled in Canada
built a strong Church there, despite great hardships and the
massacres inflicted by the Indians. When the French lost the
battle for the territory to the English, attempts were made to
introduce Protestantism, but the Catholics stood strong with
their priests, and retained the French language so as not to
lose their identity as French Catholics. Since the wave of
colonists from France stopped about 1756, while the English
kept coming, it was a difficult struggle for about 80,000 hardy
souls to keep the faith, but they never gave in, and the French
Canadian Church of today stands as a monument to their
strong faith.

A number of attempts were made by French Catholics
to evangelize the Indians. The infamous dealings of the white
traders, however, and the greed of white land-seekers were
too great obstacles to any great success.

The vast Louisiana territory, which Napoleon eventually
would sell to the United States, was another colonial strong-
hold of French Catholics. Here the French were never too
numerous, and those there led a softer life than their brothers
in Canada, but they remained loyal to their faith.

Negroes and Christianity

We have seen the spread of the Gospel of Christ among the white and yellow races, and also among the Indians of the Americas. What of the black race?

As we noted, little headway was made in Africa itself, and matters stood thus until well into the nineteenth century, when the great Dark Continent missionaries came on the scene: Bishop Lavigerie with his White Fathers and White Sisters of Africa, Venerable Father Libermann with the Congregation of the Holy Spirit, the Lyons Missionaries, and many, many others.

Protestant missionaries also evangelized many regions in this vast continent.

Africa, particularly western Africa, had a highly developed culture and a number of splendid kingdoms centuries before the discovery of America. Africans also joined the Spanish, Portuguese and French explorers and adventurers crossing the Atlantic to the New World. A black man was the pilot of Christopher Columbus' ship, the *Niña*. And one of the first explorations into the southwestern region of the United States was led by another Negro, Estevanico.

But though the first black men to walk the regions of the New World were free men, from the sixteenth to the eighteenth centuries, approximately twelve to fifteen million Africans were ruthlessly dragged to the Americas as prisoners and then sold as slaves. For them, the New World was anything but a "promised land"! Men who had been rulers, landowners, and respected members of their own country were captured by greedy white and even black slave traders, together with their women and children, herded into ships, packed so cruelly that often one third of them died during the trip, and finally sold into suffering and humiliation — for no reason but because their physical strength and endurance made them unsurpassed laborers on the plantations of North and South America. How could Christians have tolerated such an inhuman practice so long?

Sold for life

"Strangers! You were not men! You knew all the books of the world, but you did not know love!" So writes a black poet of Senegal, B. Diop.

Once the trade was established, the whole economic system became founded on it. Protests from Christian rulers as well as the heroic attempts of countless missionaries and Church leaders could not put a stop to it. They only succeeded in obtaining better treatment of the slaves. The French "Black Code" was the first legal document guaranteeing some rights to slaves. Moreover, the missionaries did all they could to keep slave families from being sold separately; they taught them the faith and built churches for them, with the Black Code guaranteeing them Sunday off from labor. They took care of the sick and the orphans among them. We have already mentioned the tremendous apostolate of St. Peter Claver in Cartagena, Colombia, on behalf of the Negro slaves.

In Central and South America, the blacks eventually became an integral part of the society, but in North America, the situation was different. The English law or custom did not recognize slavery, so the first Negroes, like countless whites from Europe, were sold as indentured servants. In the case of white men, to be an indentured servant meant that one sold his services for a certain length of time in return for payment of a debt he was unable to pay. But in the case of the blacks, men were often sold "for life." In other words, they were actually *slaves*. By 1770, there were about 697,628 Negro slaves in the thirteen colonies, most of whom were in the South, since the cotton and sugar plantations depended on their labor. As time went on the anti-slavery movement grew, and was a major issue of our Civil War. Racism and prejudice became far more serious a problem in the United States than in the French and Spanish colonies of Central and South America.

American Negroes fought with white Americans for freedom in the Revolutionary War, and in all other wars down through our history. Yet their own freedom from slavery was very slow in coming, and full, equal rights and opportunities have still not been attained in practice, though they are decreed by law.

As in South America, the blacks in general adopted the religion of the whites. While there it was the Catholic faith, in the North, it was the Protestant, for the most part, and principally Baptist and Methodist. The first colored Baptist church was opened in Savannah, Georgia, but until the emancipation of the slaves, most Negroes attended the churches of their masters. Once freed, they began to open more and more of their own separate Baptist churches.

**Bishop James Augustine Healy was a credit
to his Church and his race**

Even in the colonial period, mainly in Louisiana, there were black Catholics, and as early as 1866, the Catholic Church leaders determined to establish Negro churches and schools. The first three colored priests were the Healy brothers, sons of an Irish father and a mulatto mother. They were brilliant, holy men, one of whom became the Bishop of Maine and another, a Jesuit, the President of Georgetown College. But on the whole, the form of Christianity which claimed most Negroes was Protestant revivalism.

The French Revolution

In 1789, the French Revolution exploded. The French king and queen were put to death. Bloodthirsty mobs rounded up members of the nobility, men and women alike, to imprison them and then behead great numbers of them in public executions. Thousands of simple people, peasants and artisans, were massacred. In fact, anyone not in sympathy with the revolution was in danger of execution.

The Church suffered greatly during this *reign of terror,* because the bishops were often members of nobility; in the minds of the revolution's leaders, the Church was linked up with the king and the nobles whom they were determined to destroy. In fact, the revolution was violently anti-religious.

Convents and monasteries were forcibly closed and all religious were ordered to return to secular life. Persecution and death awaited those who resisted. It was another age of heroes and martyrs, of Mass offered in secret by priests who refused to break their loyalty to the Holy Father as the revolutionary leaders desired.

Matters grew steadily worse. Efforts increased to destroy Christianity completely. A woman symbolizing "the Goddess of Reason" was dramatically crowned in the great Cathedral of Notre Dame in Paris! Loyal priests were sent out of the country (and a number of them came to serve the Church in the United States). Revolutionary armies moved into other countries of Europe and spread their anti-religious ideas and practices.

The terrible climax came when the Pope was taken prisoner and brought to southern France! There Pius VI died a captive of the revolutionaries.

Napoleon, the little emperor

The man who dominated the next period of European affairs was the "little emperor," *Napoleon Bonaparte.* As a young general, he had marched on the papal territories in the name of the revolutionary leaders of France, but when he seized complete control of France, he was wise enough to realize that the Roman Catholic religion was stronger than ever among the people.

Once the laws against religion had been revoked, people flocked to the churches again, and those who had broken with the Pope out of fear of the revolutionaries now returned to the Church.

Everywhere new religious fervor and loyalty to the Holy Father were evident.

Pope Pius VII, however, soon realized to his great grief, how little love and respect Napoleon had for faith or anything else except his own tremendous thirst for power. After making an agreement with the Holy See, the Emperor proceeded to draw up a list of seventy-seven articles which were designed to make the Church in France subject to him in almost every way! It even contained rules about celebrating the liturgy! Of course, Pius VII could not agree to this interference in the affairs of the Church.

But Napoleon intended to let nothing stop him. Finally he went so far as to take the Pope captive, after having conquered all the lands belonging to the Church!

For five years, the Vicar of Christ was the prisoner of the French ruler, who now was master of most of Europe.

Pius VII had been a monk, and he was a man of great strength of will and courage, as well as a man of prayer. Contrary to Napoleon's expectations, therefore, he did not break down and give in to the Emperor's demands for control of the Church. Neither deceptively kind treatment nor cruel threats moved him.

"Chi tocca il Papa muore," the Italians say. This proverb means: those who lay hands on the Pope die. Napoleon himself once admitted, *"There are only two powers on earth: the sword and the spirit....In the end, the sword is always beaten by the spirit."* And so it happened. The powers of Europe finally succeeded in striking back at the self-made Emperor, and his downfall was swift.

**Two strong-willed men:
one all for self, the other all for Christ's Church**

Utterly humiliated, Napoleon was banished to the island of Elba and later to the unhealthy, bleak rock of St. Helena.

Pius VII, meanwhile, was restored to Rome amid scenes of wild joy. Respectful acclaim and love were showered on the one-time prisoner in white, the gentle, firm successor of St. Peter.

Always a father to his people, he showed himself as magnificent in forgiveness of Napoleon as he had been firm in resisting him. He welcomed many of the Emperor's family as they fled for their lives from France, and he appealed to rulers to give the Emperor himself better treatment. When Napoleon asked for a priest, the Pope personally sent one of the ex-emperor's own countrymen.

Pio Nono

After the fall of Napoleon, the papal lands were returned to the Holy See by the monarchs who met to restore Europe to the old state of affairs before the Revolution. This restoration of monarchy was not to last very long, however, for the movement toward republicanism grew stronger and stronger.

In the reign of the great Pope, Pius IX, popularly known as Pio Nono, the revolutionary movement broke out again all over Europe. This time, however, it was not as anti-religious as the French Revolution. In fact, the revolutionaries were, in many cases, fervent Catholics. Priests often joined in the struggle to obtain more representation in government by the people.

The Holy Father was the object of love, respect and devotion as never before.

Still, as it turned out, the revolution in Italy brought loss of the papal states and great suffering to Pius IX, whose reign was the longest in the history of the Church: thirty-two years.

Pius IX ascended the throne of Peter in 1846. The nationalistic movements began in 1848. Twenty-two years later, all the territories of Italy had been taken from the Holy See, as Italy's leaders moved to unite the divided peoples of that peninsula into one nation. In this Italian nationalistic movement, enemies of the Church were also involved. One leader, Garibaldi, declared that he intended to make Rome the headquarters of Freemasonry!

The Pope himself realized that it was only a matter of time before the temporal power and lands of the Church would be lost. He foresaw the trial he himself would have to endure. Yet this elderly man of unshakable valor did not retreat in any way.

At that very difficult time, in fact, he decided to call on the great spiritual strength of Christ's Church by summoning an ecumenical council. He knew that despite the threatening political situation, the loyalty of the world's Catholics to their faith and to the Vicar of Christ was perhaps stronger than ever before.

The First Vatican Council

The First Vatican Council opened December 8, 1869 and was attended by 731 Council Fathers. (Nearly one hundred years later, the Second Vatican Council Fathers numbered about two thousand!) After only seven months, this Council was interrupted by the attack of the liberals on Rome, and it was never resumed. However, it did solemnly set forth, for all to believe, the truth of faith that the Pope cannot make a mistake when he uses his supreme, apostolic authority to proclaim a doctrine of faith or morals. This teaching, of course, was by no means "new" in the Church, but now it was solemnly defined as a dogma of Faith.

Pius IX lived eight more years after Rome was taken by the new Italian Government. He strongly protested the injustice that had been done the papacy, and made himself the voluntary "Prisoner of the Vatican," refusing to go into the city of Rome itself as a sign of protest. He suffered, too, from news of persecution of Catholics in Germany, in Mexico, and in Spain, as well as from the anti-Catholic measures in Italy itself.

Yet, when he died in 1878, it was plain to see that the **Catholic Church was more alive than ever.** The loss of his lands had only served to make the Holy Father more loved than ever as the spiritual Father of *all* Catholics of every land.

**Two great truths of faith
were solemnly defined in Pius IX's reign**

Dogma of Papal Infallibility
VATICAN COUNCIL I
1870

Dogma of the Immaculate Conception of the Blessed Virgin Mary
Pope Pius IX
1854

His role as Supreme Teacher and Guide was universally recognized, and the Church enjoyed a wonderful unity that rose above all political and physical boundaries.

The suffering of the Pope and the faithful increased faith and love.

Especially important

▶ TO REFLECT ON:

In the period just studied, when their churches seemed superficial and stiff, we have seen some Christians start seeking mystical experiences.

Do you see something like that going on today?...

Don't those who take drugs, for instance, often say that the drug visions give them "kicks" that the "structural, superficial world" does not give? They "escape" to the shadow world of drugs because they think it is "more real." But as one girl who quit drugs in time said, "You don't feel able to make decisions; you get panicky and you're afraid to think of the future."

Any kind of "escape attempt" is dangerous. One expert on drug abuse warned, "Don't play Russian roulette with your mind. If you've thought about trying one of the kickers — glue sniffing, LSD, marihuana, etc. — bear in mind that along with the kicks, the whiners, and the highs comes the possibility of doing permanent damage to some part of your body, such as the brain, liver, kidney or lungs." He goes on to relate that many become permanently psychotic: "They never come down from cloud nine."

In religion and in life, it is better to play the game according to God's plans, and not go after kicks. (The real mystics don't look for visions: they seek *God*, and even when He grants visions, with them come heavy responsibilities toward others.)

Life, *real life*, cannot be based on what is artificial: drug or drink thrills, money pleasures, sex pleasures, power pleasures. You're too wonderful to fall into that kind of trap.

▶ TO STRIVE FOR:

Be real. When you're happy, great! When you've got a problem, face it. Pray, get help, *act* — but don't *exit*. Learn to handle your problems, in school, at work, in social life, in sports, in inter-personal relationships. Freedom is yours to use for fulfillment and growth. You will use it well if you never lose sight of what you mean to God, who created you out of love.

▶ TO TALK TO GOD ABOUT:

With St. Hilary of Poitiers, say:

Let me speak to You, God of all power. Even though I am
    only dust and ashes, still, since I am joined to You by
    ties of love,
    let me speak freely.

Before I came to know You, I was nothing.
I had the misfortune not to know the meaning of life.
I didn't know myself.
I was in no way what I am now.
You in Your mercy gave me life. I do not doubt in the least
    that You decided it would be good for me to be born.
For You are good. You did not need me at all. And You would
    not have given me life, if it were to be to my det-
    riment....

As long as I am alive,
as long as I breathe the breath You have given me,
Holy Father, almighty God,
I will acknowledge that You have been both God and Father
    from all eternity.

8

THE POPES AND THE WORLD

"We have seen with the greatest consolation a sight which makes the image of the Mystical Body of Jesus Christ shine with a special and significant splendor in every part of the globe.

"In spite of a prolonged internecine war, which unfortunately destroyed the fraternal community of the nations, We have seen all Our sons in Christ, wherever they are, turn with one will, one charity, one mind, toward the common Father of all....

"On all sides, Catholics, even of combatant nations, turn to the Vicar of Jesus Christ as to a most loving Father of all men...."

Pope Pius XII, 1943

"I want to be a true daughter of the Church, like our holy Mother, St. Teresa, and pray for all the intentions of Christ's Vicar. That is the one great aim of my life."

ST. THERESE OF LISIEUX

"We live in days when the soul strongly feels the need of prayer. In the tempest which is blowing over Europe, we feel the nothingness of the creature, and turn to the Creator."

CHARLES DE FOUCALD, from the Sahara Desert, 1916

In the period from the last part of the nineteenth century to the opening of World War II, the complex developments on a world-wide scale are best seen within the framework of the papacy, for the Rock of Peter constitutes the clearly visible sign of unity for the far-scattered members of the Mystical Body.

Social, economic, and political upheavals, a disastrous world war, modern heresy, as well as amazing growth in the numbers, unity and spirit of the Catholic faithful form the content of this chapter.

A weak, powerless Church?

From the Council of Trent, right down to the pontificate of Leo XIII — for three hundred years — the Church had struggled hard to retain her freedom to teach in the name of Jesus Christ. She had had to defend her faith and her God-given rights against aggressive Catholic sovereigns as well as greedy revolutionaries, against rationalism and anti-Christian thought presented in the name of science. The papal states had finally been snatched from the Church, and the pope was dead as a political power in Europe.

Indeed, the Church appeared weak and powerless in a world of freethinkers.

Yet, those who thought her days were numbered had failed to take notice of the dynamic seeds of rebirth planted in her soil by Pius IX and already evident in the upsurge of love and spiritual influence enjoyed by the Vicar of Christ. In the next century, Providence was to give the Church incomparable leaders, matchless Pontiffs, who would lead her out of isolation, make her voice heard once again, and clearer than ever, on great religious, social and moral issues.

All through the twentieth century, the world has come to look to the See of Peter for leadership in the cause of peace. The Church came "out of the catacombs" to become the center of international life and a powerful sign of liberty and unity for all mankind. At the same time, she has ever continued to fulfill her mission of leading men to salvation in fidelity to her Founder.

POPE LEO XIII

The twenty-five-year reign of Leo XIII covers the end of the nineteenth century and the beginning of the twentieth (1878-1903). When Joachim Cardinal Pecci ascended the papal throne as Leo XIII, succeeding Pius IX, those who knew this brilliant and highly experienced man rejoiced for the Church.

The profound respect he soon earned from world leaders, despite the anti-clericalism and hatred of religion which was being propagated, is evident in the number of sovereigns and political powers who called on the Vicar of Christ. Germany is a specially noteworthy case.

An anti-Catholic campaign called the *Kulturkampf,* started by Count von Bismark, had caused great hardships for German Catholics. With extreme skill, Pope Leo achieved an agreement with the German rulers, while never compromising the courageous stand of the Catholic Center Party, which had struggled successfully against Bismark's persecution. Bismark himself manifested his admiration for the Pope by asking him to settle the disagreement between Germany and Spain over the Caroline Islands.

But it was especially in the social field that Leo XIII set the Church on a new path. As we saw in the last chapter, a great number of those who fought for "liberty, progress and modern social practices" were also bitterly anti-religious. Thus liberal groups and associations of workers were often hot-beds of attacks on the Church.

In France, especially, but in other countries, too, a number of Catholics had achieved some kind of compromise between the new social views and the Church. They wanted to support the good aspects of the new movements which would help common people to unite and better their conditions, to have a say in their government. But since the leaders of the popular movements were mostly enemies of the Church, aiming to deprive the Church of all its possessions, other Catholics wanted to have nothing to do with them. This thorny problem caused much disagreement and bitterness.

La Mennais, misguided liberal

Félicité de La Mennais, (1782-1854) a French priest, is the most outstanding example of the torment of the times. He and others who took him as their leader rejected the godless liberty of the revolutionaries just as they had rejected the tyranny of supposedly Catholic rulers who were opposed to liberty. He wrote and worked to draw the Church into the revolutionary movements.

To La Mennais and his followers, the solution was simple: the Church should withdraw from the temporal world, have nothing to do with rulers, and be more or less a purely spiritual power. His newspaper, *L'Avenir (The Future),* was a mixture of fine ideas and errors, rash theories and fantastic schemes. To many, and to the Holy Father himself, this kind of movement seemed very dangerous; it looked as though it sided with the anti-Catholic revolutionaries who were struggling to strip the Church of all she possessed. As a result, La Mennais' "liberal Christianity" was condemned.

At first, the priest submitted publicly, but he soon opposed the Pope, and finally gave up both his priesthood and his faith. Had he been as humble and holy as he was energetic and determined, he might have been a great modern social apostle.

La Mennais' newspaper reflected ardent but confused plans

Alarmed by all the confusion and diversion, Pope Pius IX had flatly condemned the whole liberal movement in documents called "Quanta Cura" and "The Syllabus." Naturally, he was only condemning the "liberty and progress" slogans when used as weapons of war against religion, but it looked to many as though the Church were rejecting forever the trend toward democracy and the rise of the working classes.

Moreover, Socialism and Communism had come into being, and here again, although they proposed to help the working classes, they were doctrines full of harmful errors.

Such was the situation when Pope Leo XIII took up the problem and launched the Church into the twentieth century social world.

Champions of social justice

A number of far-sighted, social-minded Catholics had prepared the way for Pope Leo's action and collaborated with him. In Ireland, Daniel O'Connell, the great patriot, had championed the cause of freedom for the persecuted, poverty-stricken Irish Catholics, uniting them and speaking for them in the British Parliament. His forceful courage helped to win them their rights, by stirring the consciences of British leaders.

In France, Frederick Ozanam had aroused social consciousness by organizing the St. Vincent de Paul Conferences. These were groups of young men who volunteered to help the poor and make the rich aware of their needs.

In Germany, Bishop von Ketteler was another great champion of social justice, as was Toniolo in Italy. In England, Cardinal Manning's defense of workers and charity toward them won him the affectionate title of "Cardinal of the Workers."

Pope Leo began by urging Catholics in every land to organize and to take part in government so as to Christianize the new republican movements. He urged Catholic workers to band together to seek their rights from governments, not by revolution. Little by little, the Christian social parties grew stronger in Austria, Germany, Hungary, Belgium, Italy, etc., and the lot of the working classes began to improve.

"New Things"

But the greatest step Pope Leo XIII took, a step which helped to save enormous masses of working people from the slavery of Communism, was the publication of the encyclical, *Rerum Novarum*, "New Things," in May of 1891. In this monumental document, the Pope spoke up for labor unions and for the right to strike when necessary to obtain just conditions. He advocated cooperative industries run by the workers themselves, such as farmers' cooperative dairies, and cooperative banks. He urged the formation of associations of workers to improve their social and cultural conditions.

In other words, all the benefits we take for granted today were advocated by the Pope at a time when many still thought that power, education, and money should be the possessions of only a few.

Once more, the world saw the Church of Christ as the champion of what is best for man in this life, as well as in the next.

New spiritual strength

Pope Leo XIII was a very brilliant scholar, too, and he promoted progress in theology and philosophy, especially as presented by the genius Thomas Aquinas. To show the world that the Church has nothing to fear from honest research and study, he opened the secret Vatican archives (where all the documents of her long history are kept) to scholars of every religion and nation.

Greatly devoted to the Blessed Mother, the Pope made her holy Rosary a most popular devotion throughout the world. Indeed, he so clearly taught her sublime role in the Redemption and her privileges that we can call him a leading figure in the science of Mariology, or Marian studies.

Devotion to the Blessed Virgin had increased more than ever since Pius IX had solemnly defined the truth of her Immaculate Conception, which means that Mary was conceived without original sin. Four years later, in 1858, the Mother of God had appeared to St. Bernadette at Lourdes, France, and said of herself, "I am the Immaculate Conception."

Fervor and deep love for the faith were never more evident than in the Holy Year of 1900, when Rome was literally overwhelmed with floods of devout pilgrims from every part of the world. They came to receive the blessing of the Vicar of Christ and to pray in the greatest church of Christendom, the Basilica of St. Peter. Men and women of every race and nationality met to worship together, united by their love of Christ and their membership in the Church, His Mystical Body.

In the field of ecumenism, Pope Leo's wonderful personality and keen understanding helped him establish warm relations with non-Catholic Christians. At this point, we should look more closely at an amazing development in England, begun decades before, but whose central figure, John Henry Newman, was raised to the cardinalate by Pope Leo.

The Oxford Movement

John Henry Newman was a minister of the Anglican or Established Church of England. His great thirst for union with Christ and his restless search for religious truth had made him famous at Oxford University. Many intellectuals gathered around him and they published a great number of *tracts* or booklets on the true nature of the Church. Their aim was to try to reform the Anglican Church, which they considered spiritually dead.

As time went on, however, the popular scholar and preacher began to realize that the more he studied and meditated, the closer he seemed to feel to the Roman Catholic Church. Yet love and loyalty held Newman to the Church of England.

So popular was he that when the Anglican Church authorities frowned on his activities, he could easily have become the leader of a new religion. But Newman had no such ambitions. He only wanted to find the true Church.

"I was on a bed of agony," he said later, describing the years when he painfully wrenched himself away from his Church to go over to the Church he had recognized as the only true one.

October 8, 1845: John Henry Newman asked an Italian Passionist priest, Bl. Dominic Barberi, to come to his home. Before him he solemnly pronounced his abjuration of allegiance to the Established Church. The agony of indecision was over. For Newman and England, a "second Spring" had come. No one could have rejoiced more than the great Passionist priest, Bl. Dominic Barberi, whose life-long desire had been to be instrumental in bringing England back to the Church.

**Newman's light was destined
to be followed by many**

Lead, Kindly Light, Amid the encircling
gloom —
Lead Thou me on!
The night is dark and
I am far from
home.
Lead Thou me on!
Keep Thou my feet;
I do not ask to see
The distant
scene —

Over three hundred other Anglican professors and theologians followed Newman into the Catholic Church in the short space of one year! Never again would Catholicism be despised in England as the religion of the ignorant. Another brilliant Anglican clergyman, Henry Edward Manning, was asked to answer the arguments of the converts, but he, too, was led by his studies to see the Roman Catholic Church as the only true one. For five years he held back, yet in the end, he became a Catholic and was later made a Cardinal.

Cardinal Manning, the great leader and organizer, and Cardinal Newman, the famous writer and thinker, are two of the most outstanding figures of English Catholicism.

Controversy in the U. S.

On the American scene, the most famous Churchman at this period was the country's only Cardinal, James Cardinal Gibbons, Archbishop of Baltimore, Maryland. And what a swirl of controversy and opposition marked this period of stupendous growth!

Indeed, some laymen became so independent that they tried to run their parishes and actually opposed their bishops. This dangerous situation, called *trusteeism*, eventually disappeared, but the seed of discord soon showed up again in rivalry between clergy and laity of different nationalities when the great tide of immigration from Europe began.

During the reign of Pope Leo XIII, the Catholic population of the United States was tripled, going from about 4,500,000 to approximately 12,500,000. The nations which sent the most immigrants were Ireland, Germany, Italy, Austria-Hungary, Poland and Canada.

The Irish were the first to come in the largest numbers and this fact, together with their knowledge of English, brought about their rise to prominent positions in the Church. Other groups began to resent this dominance of the Irish, and there was much misunderstanding and even hostility, particularly between the Irish and German groups.

In Cardinal Gibbons the immigrants and working classes found a true friend

Three major problems are evident: the discord between Catholic immigrants of vastly different nationalities; the near-condemnation of labor unions as secret societies; and the so-called "Americanism" heresy. In all these areas, Cardinal Gibbons' masterly ability played a significant role.

Right from the start, American Catholics for the most part had represented various nationalities, and the problem of cooperation and unity was only to be expected. Moreover, this problem was increased by the fact that they were always under pressure, due to the distrust with which most non-Catholic Americans looked on the Church. The American spirit of independence, together with little knowledge of normal Church legislation and practice, also added to the difficulty of promoting unity between isolated Catholic groups spread around the country.

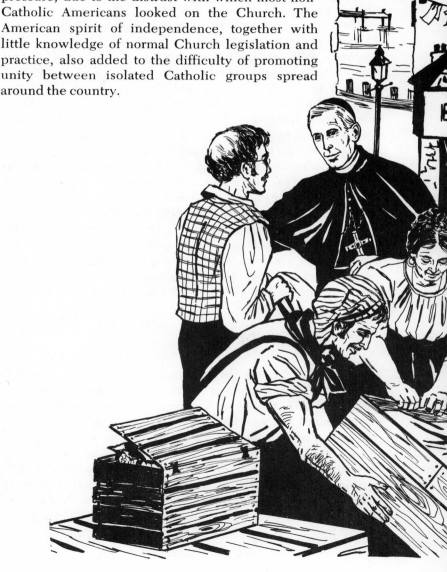

An explosive situation

To make matters worse, anti-Catholic feelings began to increase among other Americans, many of whom had grown up with mistaken ideas about Catholic belief and practice. United States history, in fact, records at various periods the existence of secret anti-Catholic societies such as the *"Know Nothings,"* the *"American Protective Association"* (born in this period, 1887) and later, the *Ku Klux Klan*. It was an explosive situation which frequently erupted in riots, campaigns of hatred, and even killings and destruction of Church property.

Still, through it all, the Church held together because of the bond of supernatural faith, as Cardinal Gibbons said. And gradually, as the children of the immigrants grew up together, the old feuds and quarrels died out. Prejudice against Catholics took longer to lose its popularity, but thanks to the far-sighted efforts of such leaders as Cardinal Gibbons and Archbishop John Ireland of St. Paul, Minnesota, the immigrants entered wholeheartedly into American life and helped dispel the ill-will by their devotion to the nation.

As Catholics cooperated together more and more, as religious orders from various nations established foundations in the United States, as new dioceses sprang up all across the land, the Church sunk its roots deep into American soil. She also began an amazing system of schools supported by the offerings of generous faithful, who on the average were far from rich and who were already burdened with the support of the churches and rectories. Every year, thousands of Americans were moved by God to seek entrance into the Church.

The Knights of Labor

That the Church in America did not lose countless numbers of workingmen was greatly due to the vision and vigorous stand taken by Cardinal Gibbons on the labor unions issue. The problem arose because of the more ancient problem of secret societies, such as Masonry, which had been so anti-Catholic. The Church had forbidden membership by Catholics in any secret society which had a religious rite opposed to Catholic belief, or which had the goal of working against lawful authority, or which used evil methods to achieve its aims.

Now the first labor groups, organized to give workingmen the power to obtain better conditions and pay, looked like secret societies, and looked, therefore, dangerous. As the first real labor union, the Knights of Labor, grew in membership and power, some American bishops asked the Holy See to forbid membership in it by Catholics. Cardinal Gibbons understood their worry, but he understood, too, that thousands of Catholics—for Catholic immigrants were nearly all workingmen—would be lost to the Church if membership in labor unions was forbidden.

On February 20, 1889, the Cardinal set forth his views in defense of the Knights of Labor, even though he knew that this action would anger the wealthy, powerful businessmen. As he later said, "If the Church did not protect the workingman, she would have been false to her whole history, and this the Church can never be."

Pope Leo XIII agreed with the judgment of the wise Cardinal, and no condemnation of the labor union ever came forth. In fact, from 1880 on, in the eyes of the American public, the Catholic Church stood forth as a champion of the workingman's rights.

Heresy in America?

"Americanism"—this word, even today, is a controversial one. To many, it stands for a heresy which developed in the U.S. at the close of the nineteenth century. Others feel that American Catholics never held the errors condemned under the term, "Americanism." How did this situation come about?

We recall that in France there was still much strife between those who supported the republic and those who longed for the return of a monarchy. Now some French writers, supporters of the republic, began to praise exaggerated reports of Catholic teaching and practice in the United States. It seemed to many that dangerous ideas were being exalted: that the Church should get rid of its moral strictness and "go soft"; that guidance from Church authorities should be dropped and one should rather do what he thought the Holy Spirit was telling him to do; that the religious virtues of poverty, chastity and obedience practiced in imitation of Christ were not as praiseworthy as active virtues.

The result was an encyclical letter by Pope Leo called *Testem Benevolentiae.* In it the Holy Father pointed out the

error in the above doctrines, while noting the confusion regarding the source or existence of these teachings. Many U.S.
Catholics, including Cardinal Gibbons, were grieved that the
name "Americanism" should be given to the errors.

As for the common European belief that Americans were
only good for action and too immature for contemplation, for
a deep spiritual life, the existence of many contemplative
convents and monasteries proved differently. Moreover, the
religious life in all its forms and apostolates flourished from
coast to coast, manifesting the evident esteem of American
Catholics for the vows of poverty, chastity and obedience as
the heroic imitation of Christ.

POPE ST. PIUS X

Joseph Sarto, who succeeded Leo XIII on the throne of
Peter as Pius X, differed from him greatly. Born of a very poor
family in the little town of Riese in North Italy, he had spent
his early priestly life in small town parishes, and had then
risen to the bishopric and cardinalate. His experience, therefore, was not in international relations, but in pastoral care of
souls. Moreover, he was an extremely humble, simple man.

As bishop, he once told a friend to stay at his mother's
house when traveling through Riese. "How will I recognize
the Sarto house?" asked the man.

"Oh," replied the bishop with a smile, "just look for a
house with purple stockings hanging out the window to dry!"
He well knew his mother's pride in her bishop-son!

Pius X's warm personality, his lovable simplicity, and his
deep saintliness soon became evident to all. It also became
apparent before long that he possessed immense practical
wisdom and extraordinary courage.

A Pope of the Twentieth Century, and a saint besides, he
had a taste for simplifying proceedings, for giving the Vatican
a more simple, modern "look" in its customs and especially in
the ceremonies of tribute to the Pope himself.

Pius X was also deeply concerned about deepening piety
and the life of the spirit. He brought about a reform in the
liturgy, especially in Church music. In many areas, the kind
of music being played and the instruments being used certainly did not serve to lift the mind to God, but rather to dis-
tract attention from the great sacrifice of the Mass.

Another custom in need of reform was the practice of receiving Holy Communion very infrequently. Pius X encour-

**The peasant Pope was both
lovable and firm**

aged very frequent, even daily, Communion, and permitted little children to receive as soon as they understood the Sacrament sufficiently.

From his long experience in parish work the Holy Father knew how much ignorance there was among the great masses of the faithful regarding Catholic teaching. For this reason, he started a great catechetical movement, ordering that the CCD (Confraternity of Christian Doctrine) be set up in every diocese of the world and that the catechism be taught without fail.

The heartaches of St. Pius X

Two immense problems that faced this great Pope were the breaking off of diplomatic relations with France and the Modernist heresy.

Pope Leo XIII had done his best to avoid a break with the anticlerical government of France, but this government continued to show hostility to the Church. When matters came to a head, and the State broke relations with the Vatican, it also took for itself all the property of the Church, deprived the clergy of support, and attempted to withdraw them from obedience to the Holy Father.

Despite the disapproval of the fearful, who considered him undiplomatic, Pope Pius X urged the priests of France to break with the hostile government. He was absolutely confident of their faith and loyalty, and he was not mistaken. United in a common spirit of sacrifice and courage, they remained faithful to the Church and its Vicar, whose heart was broken by this painful conflict but whose spirit was as strong as ever.

Modernism represented the saintly Pope's second great trial. This hard-to-describe heresy had filtered into so many areas and deceived so many, even brilliant men and priests, that it seemed almost impossible to pin it down. Philosophy, theology, Bible study, social theories — all were becoming tainted with the Modernist views which watered down the teachings of Christ to "suit" certain modern tastes. What added to all the confusion was the fact that the ideas were spread indirectly through reviews, books, addresses and newspapers. For many, they appeared to be just new trends, "signs of progress" — not heresy.

To attack all this directly was apt to make the Pope look like an enemy of modern approaches, like a slow conservative unable to keep up with the times, like a tyrant using heavy-handed tactics to stop "the best thing going" — according to the supporters of Modernism.

A saint is never a coward, never a slave to popularity polls. And Pius X, the peasant Pope, was a genuine saint, who loved the Church and souls as much as he loved Christ. So he plunged fearlessly into the midst of the turmoil to root up the heretical movement, publishing three basic documents in 1907 alone. In these he exposed the fundamental errors so clearly and strikingly that the poisonous movement was brought out into the open. Thus, by the end of his life, seven years later, the true Catholic faith was safe.

1914 saw the tragic outbreak of the First World War. Pius X, who knew so well what sufferings war would bring, who had refused to bless the weapons that would make Eu-

rope run with blood, was crushed under the weight of the
sorrow. The man who had not bent under personal attack
died of grief at this blow to humanity.

POPE BENEDICT XV

The new Pope, Giacomo Della Chiesa, who took the name
of Benedict XV, faced the dreadful spectacle of a war-torn
Europe. France and Belgium had already been invaded and
parts of the Balkan countries were in flames. The Holy Father
knew that the Church had a major part to play in working for
peace and in lessening the horrors and hatred of war.

Indeed, the Cardinals who had elected him had dramatically shown the watching world what a bond of unity the
Christian faith can be. For although many had come from
nations fighting each other — Cardinal Mercier of Belgium, for
example, had heroically resisted the German invaders — still
they had met in a unity that overcame national feelings. And
in admirable harmony they had elected the two hundred fifty-
eighth successor to St. Peter.

The Pope's efforts and proposals for bringing about an
end to the hostilities met with the criticism of those who were
opposed to religion and did not want the Church to have any

**The charity of Christ's Vicar
toward the war's victims**

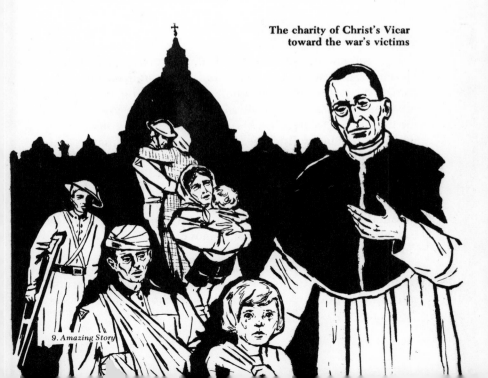

9. Amazing Story

say. Undiscouraged, Benedict turned the Vatican into an international center of charity. Help was sent to starving regions; negotiations were made for the exchange of prisoners of war; brief "cease-fire" periods were brought about by papal action; missing persons were located, and correspondence was handled between prisoners and their distant families. So magnificent was the Holy Father's charity, during the war and in the very difficult post-war period that the entire world looked on the See of Peter with tremendous respect and admiration. Christ certainly provided His Church with extraordinary Vicars for the complex Twentieth Century.

Benedict XV continued the important works begun by St. Pius X, and added many of his own. One field in which he did much concerned Eastern Christians. In this regard, he was a forerunner of the great ecumenical figures of our day. He wanted Western Catholics to appreciate the marvelous heritage received from saints and scholars and the beautiful liturgical rites of which Eastern Catholics and Eastern Orthodox Christians can be proud. He wanted to make it absolutely clear that Catholics of the Oriental (or Eastern) rites are not "second-class citizens" in the Church, but are one, in equal rights, with Western (or Latin rite) Catholics.

After only eight years of intense labors, Pope Benedict died rather suddenly in January of 1922.

POPE PIUS XI

At the name of Achille Ratti, Pope Pius XI, people think at once of Fascism, Nazism, and Communism, the dread threats to peace and freedom, with which he had to deal.

Pius XI, however, could also be called the great Pope of the missions. To be sure, the near-miraculous growth of the missions had begun long before, back in the last quarter of the nineteenth century. But it was Pius XI and his successors who did so much to ensure the permanence of the Church in new lands by urging the formation of native priests and bishops.

It was truly wise of Pius XI to appoint African, Asian and Oriental bishops, for the Church no longer seems a "foreign" institution in a land when it is governed locally by fellow countrymen.

The success of mission activity from 1878 on can be seen by looking at the figures: in 1800 there were only about four million Catholics in all the immense territories called mission

lands; about one hundred fifty years later, with fewer countries still designated as mission territory, there were around
fifty million Catholics. From the frozen North to the great
continent of Australia, from the East to the West, the Church
was growing steadily.

The religious orders

One of the reasons for the growth of the missions is undoubtedly the "new spring" of religious communities. To
give an idea of the "population explosion" in the sisterhoods,
for example, we compare the handful of nuns—less than
fifty—in mission lands in 1800 with the 60,000 one hundred
fifty years later.

Under the patronage of St. Paul,
two twentieth-century apostles
founded religious congregations dedicated to
the mass media apostolate

Both masculine and feminine religious orders had fallen off greatly in membership by the opening of the nineteenth century, mainly because of the persecution by the revolutionaries. The Benedictine priests, for example, nearly died out entirely, but in the second half of the nineteenth century they began to grow in numbers again. The Vincentians had dwindled down to only a couple hundred members, but by the twentieth century they numbered several thousand. The Jesuits, after the society was restored by Pope Pius VII, increased so quickly in numbers that by the 1960's there were over thirty-five thousand of them. The women religious became still more numerous, far outnumbering the men.

New congregations of both men and women religious came into being, most of them international in spirit, establishment and membership. They, too, grew rapidly, and served the world in new areas of apostolate. The Salesian priests and sisters of St. John Bosco, for instance, number over 40,000 and have found many new ways of bettering the lives of young people. The Society of St. Paul and the Daughters of St. Paul, founded by Very Rev. James Alberione in 1915, are dedicated to the modern communications apostolate, using press, radio, films, television, records, and tapes to bring men closer to God. And many of the older orders began to move into new fields, such as care of the mentally retarded, rehabilitation of prisoners, and other apostolates geared to especially modern needs.

The tremendous witness of the thousands upon thousands of religious priests, brothers, and sisters striving for closer imitation of the poor, chaste, obedient Christ, and laboring for men of all races and creeds, certainly is dramatic proof of how alive the Church is!

Mexico's age of martyrs

Pius XI was Pope of the Missions, diplomat of the first degree, the first Pope to speak to the world's Catholics over the Vatican's very own radio station, set up by radio's inventor, Marconi. He was the Pope who gave married couples guidance and noble directives in a famous encyclical on marriage. He wrote another famous document on modern labor problems, and still another on motion pictures.

It was Pius XI who appealed to the world on behalf of Mexican Catholics who were undergoing a bloody persecution for their faith, and he succeeded in obtaining a gradual

Disguised, hunted by the Church's persecutors, Father Pro continued his bicycle ministry

lessening of their government's hostility toward religion.

Mexico had always been a devout Catholic country, favored in its early Christian days with the apparition of the Blessed Virgin Mary to a poor peasant, Juan Diego. But in 1857 and again in 1917, anti-Catholic leaders had determined to wipe out the Faith entirely. The only hope of survival was to "go underground," worshiping in secret. Heroic priests, religious and lay people—especially the "Cristeros," young Catholics of the resistance movement—kept the Faith alive at the risk of their lives. Many were martyred.

The most famous martyr was the witty, music-loving Jesuit, Miguèl Augustine Pro, whose courage was incredible and whose tomb is uninterruptedly visited by the thousands devoted to his memory. Ironically enough, to reach Father Pro's grave, visitors have to pass by the unattended monument over the tomb of Plutarco Calles, the professed Christ-hater who hoped to destroy Catholicism in Mexico.

The encyclical of Pius XI called attention on the plight of the Mexican people, and Calles' successors gradually decreased their persecution.

Vatican City State

It was with Fascism and Nazism that Pius XI faced his greatest struggle, for both the dictators of Italy and Germany were a great threat to the rights of man and the rights of God and his Church. However, at the beginning of his reign, relations with Italy started off better than they had ever been since the stormy seizing of the papal territories. Benito Mussolini, dictator of Italy, had realized that the country's controversy with the Church had to be settled if his energetic efforts to build up the nation were to be achieved.

Secret negotiations were begun and ended happily in the Lateran Treaty, in 1929, with a concordat between Italy and the Vatican, such as existed between the Vatican and other countries. (In fact, at the death of Pius XI, thirty-six nations of the world had official diplomatic representatives at the Holy See.)

**Pius XI sought to warn men against
the dangers of Fascism, Nazism and Communism**

The most striking result of the settlement was the creation of the *Vatican City State*. Though the smallest state in the world, a miniature country of only a little over one hundred acres, its importance is beyond measure. As ruler of an independent state, the Pope is entirely free of all interference from the Italian government, even though Vatican City is right in the middle of Rome. The nations of the world immediately recognized this sovereign, independent state known as Vatican City, thus giving it a place in the international community.

Vatican City has its own policemen and guards, its own currency, flag and seal, together with its own postal, telegraph, and telephone systems. This guarantees the Holy Father freedom and privacy in his contacts with the world. As a permanently neutral state, Vatican City is recognized by all nations as extremely important in promoting peace. Today, about fifty countries maintain permanent diplomatic relations with it.

The Pope's main purpose in creating the Vatican City State was to provide the Holy See with absolute independence for its spiritual action. It was an extremely wise and fortunate step. In fact, in the very lifetime of Pius XI himself, it proved a great blessing, for Italy soon became involved in World War II.

The dictatorships

Mussolini's efforts to bring greater development and prosperity to Italy, to lift the educational level of the people, to provide more job opportunities, led to his great personal popularity. Like Hitler in Germany, when he spoke, he had the power to sway the masses. Gradually both Italy and Germany became totalitarian states, that is, countries in which total power is given to the rulers, with the people becoming mere puppets in their hands.

The Fascist government in Italy was in the hands of the dictator Mussolini, and Nazi Germany was ruled by the iron will of the dictator Adolf Hitler.

Pius XI, the Pope of Catholic Action, had organized great movements of the lay people, especially among the young people of Italy. In the 1930's, Mussolini tried to break up the Catholic Youth Movement and then to restrict the other lay organizations more and more. The Pope responded at once, firmly defending their right to independent action. Unafraid of the consequences, he opposed every step the dictator took against the rights of the Church.

In 1931, Pius XI condemned the Fascist interference in religious matters with the encyclical, *Non abbiamo bisogno.* An American priest, Francis Spellman, who later became Cardinal Archbishop of New York, was the one who managed to get the encyclical out to the newspapers of the world, for the Fascists tightly controlled all the communications media.

(No wonder that after this, the Pope had Marconi build the powerful Vatican radio!) For a while, Mussolini let matters ride, but once he entered into an alliance with Hitler, the opposition began again.

With Germany, in order to protect the rights of the Church, the Pope had signed a Concordat through the efforts of Archbishop Pacelli. This holy, diplomatic priest had been in charge of the revision of Church law under Pope St. Pius X and had run the Vatican's war relief charities under Benedict XV; he was to become Pius XI's successor on the throne of St. Peter.

No sooner was the treaty signed, however, when the Nazi regime (German National Socialism) proceeded to break every one of its agreements. The Nazi Gestapo police silenced all who tried to protest the persecution of Christianity. The horror of Nazism was its preaching of the theory of a "master race," destined to rule everyone else, and its attempt to make itself a substitute for religion.

On March 14, 1937, Pius XI exposed the errors of Nazism in the powerful encyclical *Mit Brennender Sorge*.

Communism

Still another totalitarian government was attacking the fundamental freedoms and rights of man. This was *Communism*. In Russia, Spain and Mexico, it was responsible for terrible persecutions against the Church. Communism, indeed, is opposed to all religion, and for this reason, is generally called *Atheistic Communism*. It developed from the writings of Karl Marx, who had appealed to the working classes to unite for revolution, and from the philosophers Engels and Feuerbach.

Right from the start, Communism had set out to destroy the Church, which it considered the strongest obstacle to its goal of making men deny God and deny man his personal freedom. The Communist is supposed to be an obedient slave to his Party, exhaust himself to stir up a revolution so that existing governments will collapse, and then bring Communism into power.

The Communist dictatorship, with its reign of terror, police rule, and mass murders, is claimed to be temporary: it is supposed to "wither away and let the people rule themselves in perfect happiness, everyone owning everything, in a kind of earthly paradise (a heaven on earth)."

The obvious fact is that wherever they move into power, the Communist dictators show no signs of intending to "wither away." Instead, they reduce the people to a pathetic slavery and misery behind an iron curtain that blocks out all freedom.

On March 19, 1937, Pius XI published the famous encyclical, *Divini Redemptoris,* against atheistic Communism. This was only five days after the publication of his document on Nazism, and it was the work of a very sick man, whose tremendous concern for God's people drove him to do all in his power to prevent loss of human lives and freedom.

Especially important

▶ TO REFLECT ON:

Millions of Jews were put to death by the Nazis for no other reason than that they were Jews! This was the terrible result of the false doctrines which the Pope had condemned!

A Jewish jeweler in Massachusetts, who came to the U.S. after World War II, has indelibly impressed on his mind the horrible memory of the Nazi SS troops gunning down innocent victims before his eyes. Studded into the belts of those soldiers were the words: "God is with us!"

To what god did such a slogan witness?...

No wonder that on this subject, Pope Pius XI did not hesitate to write: "Only superficial minds can lapse into the heresy of speaking of a national God, of a national religion; only such can make the mad attempt of trying to confine within the boundaries of a single people, within the narrow blood stream of a single race, God the creator of the world, the king and lawgiver of all peoples before whose greatness all peoples are small as a drop in the bucket." (*Mit Brennender Sorge*)

We all must be very careful not to "appropriate God" to serve our private interests, to "get Him on our side" to win an argument, to make us feel superior to others. We have to remember that He will ever be on the side of fair play and love.

▶ TO STRIVE FOR:

"*I light myself up with infinity,*" wrote the modern Italian poet, Joseph Ungaretti. Try to expand your mind, through an open attitude toward others, through a willingness to appreciate their good points, to accept them on equal footing with you. Like your Church, be supra-racial, supra-national, united with all men in Christ. This is to keep to the true Christian spirit.

▶ TO TALK TO GOD ABOUT:

Father, You have no preferences.
Help me to look on everybody as my brothers and sisters.
    I have such a fear of being lost in the crowd! That is
    why I keep aloof sometimes.
Pull open my heart, so that from now on,
    nothing
    neither race nor nationality
    neither social level nor money power
    will hold me off from mixing in.
Christ, my Brother and my God, make me love my
    brothers, respect them, pray for them, stand up for
    them, play with them, find You in them.

Jesus, Redeemer of all men, begotten by the Father,
    equal in glory, before the light began,
You are the true Light, the Splendor of the Father.
You are our eternal hope.
Hear the prayers of Your servants, lifted to You from all
    over the world.
...from the glory of the Father You came down to earth
    for our salvation.
The heavens, the earth, the sea, and all that the universe
    contains hails the Author of the new salvation with a
    new song!
And we, too,
    washed in the tide of Your blood
    shout our song of glory...

FROM THE CHRISTMAS LITURGY

9

PROMOTERS
OF
PEACE
AND
GOOD
WILL

"The Catholic and Apostolic Church is mother and teacher of all nations, whose light illumines, sets on fire, inflames. Her warming voice, filled with heavenly wisdom, reaches out to every age."

Pope John XXIII

"**Pope Pius XII** was a friend of our time. He systematically opened the dialogue with all forms of modern life by applying the criterion for solving present-day problems: with the goodness and truth of the Gospel."

POPE PAUL VI

"Armed with the humility and calm which surrounded his earliest days, **Pope John** brought compassion and an understanding drawn from wide experience to the most decisive problems of a tumultuous age. He was the chosen leader of world Catholicism, but his concern for the human spirit transcended all boundaries of belief or geography."

JOHN F. KENNEDY

The Church in the mid-twentieth century has had to face the threat of three "isms" — Nazism, Fascism, and Communism. Pope Pius XII skillfully defended her from their errors while making the Church a trusted center of brotherhood, peace and wise guidance for modern man in all fields. Pope John XXIII won hearts and promoted good will with extraordinary success. Through his efforts and the Second Vatican Council which he decided to hold, a new wave of religious fervor swept the world.

POPE PIUS XII

Pius XI died rather suddenly on February 10, 1939, and Eugenio Cardinal Pacelli, elected to succeed him, took up the grave burdens of Christ's Vicar with the name of Pope Pius XII. He was a well-known figure internationally, having visited many countries as a Cardinal, including the United States. He was a renowned scholar, a modern, forward-thinking churchman who was to write and speak on just about every topic of interest to the contemporary world.

World War II

Three days after Pius XII was crowned "Servant of the Servants of God" before an enormous crowd in St. Peter's Square, Hitler hurled his armies into Czechoslovakia. Soon the devastating full-scale war which Pius XI had tried so hard to stop unleashed its fury on the world.

Pius XII, too, attempted to propose peace terms to the warring nations, but, as he expected, they were not accepted. Germany, Italy, and later, Japan were lined up against the Allied Powers, that is, the United States, Canada, England, France, Russia and others. Many nations of Europe were invaded by the Nazis and many areas in the South Pacific by the Japanese before the tide of war turned.

Hitler and Mussolini tried to win the Pope to their side by their opposition to Communism, when Communist Russia joined the Allies in 1941. Pius XII, however, was undeceived; he knew they were hoping to use him to win for themselves the favorable opinion of the rest of the world. The Pope opposed the evils of all three "isms" — Nazism, Fascism, and Communism — as enemies of the rights of God and man.

Pius XII and the persecuted Jews

Again, as in the First World War, from the throne of Peter an incessant appeal for peace came forth. And once again, the Vatican became the center of tremendous war relief services. The homeless, the refugees of various nations, and especially the hunted Jews, victims of the Nazi persecution, found shelter in St. Peter's. Since the Vatican was neutral territory

**Pius XII, the Angelic Shepherd,
calmed the terror-stricken during a raid**

and since word of the Pope's great charity gave hope to the Jews all over Europe, for whom capture meant death in the gas chambers, throngs of them pressed into the tiny State.

Pius XII welcomed them all, and even paid gold in ransom for those who had been captured. The majestic rooms of all the Vatican buildings and even the papal summer residence at Castelgandolfo were full of frightened, weary men, women and children. Perhaps never as then did the Catholic Church impress thousands of non-Catholics with the exquisite universality of her love for men.

Rome was bombed, since it was the capital of one of the fighting nations, and the terror-struck city saw its Bishop comforting the crowds in the devastated areas. Pius XII labored hard to have Rome declared an open city and finally succeeded. Thus the bomb danger was averted and the work of charity went ahead.

The Church of Silence

The war finally came to an end in 1945, but the post-war period could certainly not be called an era of peace. Atheistic Communism emerged at once as a new, or rather now open, threat to all hope for freedom and peace. Catholic countries, such as Poland, Hungary and Czechoslovakia, were once again subjugated completely to a totalitarian rule and to fierce persecution of their religion.

East Germany, and in particular East Berlin, became world-famous symbols of the fate of all captive peoples behind the Iron Curtain, as East Germans frantically dug tunnels, hurled themselves against barbed wire fences and even hijacked trains to escape into free West Berlin and West Germany.

The "Communist Paradise" is obviously far from being a paradise either in Russia itself, or in Red China or in any other Marxist-dominated land.

The Church behind the Iron or the Bamboo (Chinese) Curtain is called the "Church of Silence" because her normal life has been completely choked off. All her bishops are either killed, jailed or effectively silenced; her clergy and religious imprisoned, tortured or sent to work camps; her churches and schools closed; her most courageous lay leaders killed or exiled; and her little children taken from their parents as infants to be brought up in atheistic schools.

Cardinal Mindszenty of Hungary became a celebrated symbol of courageous resistance despite torture and brain-washing. Dearly loved by his people, he was freed when the Hungarians revolted against their oppressors, but the revolt was speedily and bloodily put down by Russian tanks. Cardinal Mindszenty was given refuge in the American embassy in Budapest, the capital, remaining there as a living protest against the Communist suppression of human rights.

In the early fifties, the Communists of North Korea provoked the Korean War, and next, Americans found themselves involved in the Vietnam war, again because of Communist aggression. The Communists gained power in Cuba, and in Latin American countries, as well as in many other areas, including the United States. Communist Party members are actively working to bring about the goals set down by Moscow — intended to lead ultimately to the triumph of the atheistic, totalitarian, communist state.

Modern martyrs

The ferocity with which the Reds attack the Church wherever they go and the efforts they make to replace it with a schismatic Church that will be their docile tool to gradually destroy religion, proves how well they recognize that the Rock of Peter is the defender of freedom, protector of the rights of God and man.

In China, especially, their persecution—both physical and psychological—of priests and heroic lay apostles, many belonging to the Legion of Mary, knew no bounds. The foreign missionaries were expelled, but the vast majority of priests in the country were native Chinese. All those who held firmly to unity with the Vicar of Christ suffered persecution. How many martyrs in the Church of Silence!

The witness they give by their resistance to all kinds of pressure and by their Christian love is incalculably precious. Writes a nun who survived the Communist enforced death-march in North Korea, in which the intrepid Maryknoll Bishop Patrick James Byrne died:

Modern examples of heroic faith

"During our time in the prison camp the officers and guards often tried to indoctrinate us with Communist ideas, but always without success. I wonder if we had any influence on them: God alone knows. Certain it is that they watched us continually. Our behavior, our patience, the charity we showed toward each other, the heroic deaths they witnessed — all this must have made a greater impression on them than their lectures and interrogations made on us.

"May all our sufferings, united to those of Christ our Redeemer, one day obtain for them the grace of conversion."

About twenty documents came from the pen of Pope Pius XII on the Communist persecution of the Church, on the sad state of that part of the Christian community whose "hands are bound and whose lips are closed." His appeal to the world when the Hungarian uprising was so ruthlessly crushed was an entirely new step in papal procedure. In that appeal he cried out: "Can the world allow itself to be indifferent to the lot of our brothers and abandon them to the fate of a degrading slavery? Surely the Christian conscience cannot escape the moral obligation of trying by every permissible means to restore their dignity and give them back liberty."

The progress of the spirit

Pius XII's long reign in the throne of St. Peter was certainly marked by suffering, but the Church in this era was also progressing toward greater penetration of marvelous mysteries of faith.

Toward the end of the Holy Year 1950, in the immense Square of St. Peter, before a thousand bishops, the entire diplomatic corp representing nearly fifty nations, and a vast crowd from all over the world, Pius XII proclaimed the dogma of the Blessed Virgin's Assumption into heaven. This truth of the faith was commonly held but now, in response to innumerable requests, it was formally defined.

Four years later, the Pope proclaimed a "Marian Year" which brought renewed devotion and great progress in *Mariology*, which is the theological study of Mary's role in our Redemption.

The rich, profound concept of the Church as Christ's *Mystical Body* was fully developed by Pius XII in the famous encyclical, "Mystici Corporis." In another encyclical, he gave scholars greater freedom than ever before and hearty encouragement to plunge deeper into biblical studies in relation to modern developments in that field.

In still another monumental work, "Mediator Dei," Pius XII began the great liturgical renewal which was to blossom forth in all its splendor in the Second Vatican Council. His encyclical "Sacra virginitas," set forth the sublime value of a total consecration of the whole person to Christ through the vow of chastity. The encyclical "Orientales Ecclesias" was one among many documents on the unity of the Church and on our separated brethren.

Great numbers of young men and women swelled the ranks of religious orders, as we have seen. But there was also a considerable number of extraordinary lay people who did not become religious but desired a life of perfection while remaining in the secular world. For them, Pius XII gave his approval to a new type of life called *secular institutes,* whose lay members profess poverty, chastity and obedience but have no real community life.

The field of the mass media of communications held the Holy Father's interest and concern, too, as is proved by his encyclical, "Miranda prorsus," the forerunner of the Second Vatican Council's "Decree on the Media of Social Communication."

On many pressing questions

Pius XII was admittedly a man of genius, as well as a saintly priest and a tireless, selfless worker. In addition to his many encyclicals, he addressed the countless groups of specialists in every field who came to him at St. Peter's to hear his words on pressing, controversial questions. So it was that he gave guidance on marriage, birth, and medical questions; on racial, political, and social problems; he spoke brilliantly on atomic energy, on geophysics and astrophysics, on sports, on peace, and on democracy.

Thousands passed through the great reception rooms of the Vatican and conversed with the Supreme Pontiff in their own languages, for Pius XII spoke a great many languages fluently. Heads of state, men of science, artists, athletes, movie stars, military leaders, business magnates — all who passed through Rome made it a point to seek an audience with the Holy Father.

A special performance by the famous Harlem Globetrotters

In 1954, Pius XII fell gravely ill and all hope of recovery disappeared. Then, quite suddenly and for no reason the doctors could discern, his condition improved. Before very long, he was back in the full swing of his exhausting duties. But four years later, on October 6, he fell mortally ill again, and died October 9 mourned by all men of good will.

POPE JOHN XXIII

The successor of Pope Pius XII was Angelo Cardinal Roncalli, who took the name of John XXIII. His election came as quite a surprise to the world, for he was not too well known universally, although he was held in high esteem by those who knew how he had handled difficult posts in Bulgaria, Greece, Constantinople and Paris. Because of his advanced age, there was some talk of John XXIII as an "interim Pope," by which the gossipers meant that his would probably be a short-term pontificate, quite unspectacular and uneventful.

But wrong they were. John XXIII soon showed everyone that he was extremely active and enterprising—daring in fact. Moreover, his warmth and good humor, his lovableness and amazing appeal, made him immensely popular. Non-Catholics, non-Christians, non-believers almost began to look on St. Peter's as a "second home," so affable was this Pope toward them.

It was even whispered by Catholics—with evident pride in their Holy Father—that more non-Catholics got to talk with him than they did!

Like Pope St. Pius X, John XXIII had begun life a poor peasant lad, and like him, too, he had retained his admirable simplicity, which disarmed even the most sophisticated. To the surprise of all, the Pope began to "go calling," making surprise visits here and there—to a children's hospital, to a jail, to a poor parish.... *Good Pope John* was the affectionate title given him spontaneously. He would not wait for people to come to him: he went to them.

The farm boy from the unknown village became a universally loved father

Pope John loved to stop to talk to people, the "little people." He said to an American photographer who had just snapped his photo: "Would you send me the picture? No one ever sends me any pictures." Recalling his army service, he once said to a captain of the Swiss Guard, "I should defer to you. I was only a sergeant!"

He was a man of a thousand jests. Once he was asked: "How many people are working in Vatican City?" Without hesitation, the Pope answered, "About half." On another occasion, pointing to the Monsignor who was acting as his interpreter, he said, "He is my teacher. I am the best pupil in his English class." Smiling all over, he added, "Know why? I am the only one he has."

In an audience with former President Dwight Eisenhower, Pope John was handed the formal speech prepared for him in English out of deference for the distinguished guest.

**Everyone found a place
in Pope John's great heart**

He glanced at the text he was supposed to read, hesitated, and then, smiling, said in Italian, "This is gonna be a beaut!" When his remark was translated, Eisenhower threw back his head and roared with laughter. The Pope joined in and the photographers snapped their pictures for the whole world to see.

The secret of Pope John

Behind all this good humor and human goodness lay the secret of Pope John's marvelous personality: his close union with Christ. The diary he kept for many years, jotting down his thoughts, reveals his great heart and soul. Here are some significant excerpts from it during the period of his pontificate:

"A well-prepared Confession made weekly on Friday or Saturday is the solid foundation upon which to work out one's sanctification. This practice keeps one ready to die a good death at any hour and moment of the day. My calm and readiness to leave and present myself to the Lord at any instant seems to me such a pledge of trust and love as to merit from that Jesus, whose Vicar on earth I am, an abundance of His mercy."

"In front of the Lord I am dust, a sinner: I live through the mercy of Jesus to which I owe all and from which I expect all. I submit myself to Him even to the point of letting myself be completely transformed by His sorrows and sufferings in the fullest abandonment of absolute conformity to His Will. Now more than ever, as long as I live, and in all things: *Obedience and Peace*."

"I feel the weight of my office and I tremble, knowing myself to be weak and frail. But I place my trust in Christ Crucified, and His Mother and look toward eternity."

"I must guard against the audacity of those fools who, intellectually blind or tricked by hidden pride, presume to do great things in the Church without having been called by God—as if our Divine Redeemer had need of their miserable cooperation, or that of any man."

"We are comforted and strengthened in the security of obeying the good and mighty Will of God."

The Second Vatican Council

"During the first conversation of the morning of January 20, 1959, with my Secretary of State," wrote Pope John in his diary, "there came to my lips the words ecumenical council, diocesan synod, and the recasting of the Code of Canon Law, without my ever having thought of them before, and contrary to every one of my thoughts and considerations on these points. The first to be surprised by my proposal was I myself; and it was never suggested to me by anyone."

Five days later, on the feast of the Conversion of St. Paul, Pope John announced his intention to call an ecumenical council, the first in nearly a century.

The Second Vatican Council was undoubtedly the supreme accomplishment of his brief pontificate. It opened on October 11, 1962, in an unforgettable ceremony which saw about two thousand bishops from all over the world filing prayerfully into St. Peter's with the Bishop of bishops, deeply moved, in their midst.

Some of the objectives of the Council were to heal the wounds of a divided Christendom, to initiate an inner renewal of the Church in all its beauty, and to further the cause of Christian unity and brotherhood among all men.

Unity was the great goal of Good Pope John's labors. For the first time in the history of ecumenical councils, the representatives of other religions were invited to be present as observers. Every possible opportunity was offered them to see at close range the entire proceedings of every meeting.

Again, for the first time in four hundred years, a department was established within the Vatican for better relations between all Christians. Pope John had it named the Secretariate for the Promotion of Christian Unity, and he described it as "a special sign of esteem and affection for separated Christians." To the third assembly of the World Council of Churches (Non-Catholic Christian Churches) in 1961, he sent Vatican observers.

Pope John also sponsored new contacts with communistic nations in the hope of advancing the cause of world peace. In March of 1963 he received the daughter and son-in-law of Premier Khrushchev of Russia in an audience, and this visit seemed to be a practical demonstration of what could be normally done to relieve world tensions.

"Mater et Magistra" and "Pacem in Terris"

In the four and a half years of his reign, Pope John issued eight encyclical letters. The first four, all written in 1959, revealed the wide variety of his fatherly concerns: Christian unity and world peace; the formation of saintly, obedient, zealous priests; the devout recitation of the Rosary; and the training of native clergy in mission lands.

July, 1961, saw the publication of *Mater et Magistra* (Christianity and Social Progress). In it he wrote that it is the duty of the wealthy nations of the world to help underdeveloped peoples and end "their state of poverty, misery and hunger." He gave recognition to the arrival of social welfare as a permanent part of the program of various governments, and spoke of 'regulated' socialization. He also pleaded for a reemphasis of the beauty and dignity of farm life.

Amounting to almost 25,000 words, *Mater et Magistra* was hailed by sociologists everywhere, who predicted that it would exert a profound influence on the Church's role in social and economic life.

One of its most remarkable features was the extraordinary stir it created among non-Catholics and its impact on the world of politics and economics. The text was frequently cited during debates in the United Nations Economic and Social Council. Excerpts were distributed by the European Economic Community, and newspapers of every continent reported and commented on it.

Pope John's last encyclical was *Pacem in Terris* (Peace on Earth), issued in April of 1963. This truly momentous document captured the imagination and sympathy of the civilized world. Never before in the history of modern times had any papal document created such instantaneous and world-wide repercussions. Political and religious leaders hailed the 100,000 word encyclical as a document of extraordinary scope and significance and supported the Pope's call for a "personal contribution from all men for world peace, regardless of race, religion or politics."

Published purposely on Holy Thursday, this letter to mankind emphasized the words of Christ at the Last Supper: "Love one another." It called for the settlement of controversy through meetings and negotiations. It exhorted the nations to overcome racial and national barriers. It pleaded

**Two months before his death
came the great encyclical on world peace**

for general disarmament among the world powers—all with a view to human freedom and human dignity.

After commenting on *Pacem in Terris* and praising it, President John F. Kennedy said, "This encyclical of Pope John makes me proud to be a Catholic."

John XXIII brought the Church, through his encyclicals and addresses, into the midst of the chaotic conditions of the twentieth century. And to every problem about which he wrote or spoke, he brought the gentle wisdom and warm love that illumined his entire life.

In November of 1962, Good Pope John fell ill, but it was not until the following spring that he really began to fail. His illness was revealed as a tumor, and his last days were days of sheer agony. The whole world assisted at his bedside, so to speak, with and for him.

"Don't worry about me," he said to his doctors. "My bags are packed and I'm ready to go." He died on June 3, 1963, voicing the hope that his death would win blessings for the Church, for the ecumenical council, and for peace.

Especially important

▶ TO REFLECT ON:

Pope John's life is proof that the "hidden virtues," the constant, unnoticed faithfulness to duty, the lovable traits of good humor, kindness and simple humility—all these make a Christian through whom Christ will work, sooner or later, in a wonderful way.

Without that spirit of prayer and obedience, without the willingness to listen to others, to show understanding, to work hard at ordinary, unspectacular jobs—without all these inner virtues, in other words, very little lasting good will come, even from much activity, planning and publicity.

▶ TO STRIVE FOR:

Be a *doer*, but a wise one, willing to do the ground-work required for success. Be willing to study, to seek and take good advice; be practical and concrete in your planning, whether it be for some temporary form of apostolate or for your life's work. If it will be an important contribution to ease spiritual and temporal needs, then it demands more of you than mere protest, talk, or hasty actions. Be willing to *work* patiently for what is important to you.

▶ TO TALK TO GOD ABOUT:

O God,
give us *serenity*
to accept
what cannot be changed,
courage to change
what can be changed,
and *Your wisdom*
to know the one
from the other.

"All this rich teaching [of Vatican II] is channeled in one direction: the service of mankind, of every condition, in every weakness and need. The Church has, so to say, declared herself the servant of humanity, at the very time when her teaching role and her pastoral government have, by reason of the council's solemnity, assumed greater splendor and vigor. The idea of service has been central."

Pope Paul VI, closing speech, Vatican II

10
THE COUNCIL AND AFTER

The Church knows that it is the seed, the leaven, the salt of the world. It sees clearly enough the astounding newness of modern times, but with frank confidence, it stands upon the path of history and says to men: "I have that for which you search, that which you lack."

POPE PAUL VI

Pope Paul VI reminds me of St. Paul. St. Paul burned with a desire to travel the entire world in order to make Christ known.

JEAN GUITTON, lay auditor at the Second Vatican Council

With the election of Pope Paul VI, the Church was given a leader who followed in the footsteps of his ecumenical-minded Predecessor. Vatican II was continued and promulgated major documents that would have a tremendous impact on almost every area of the Church's life.

The post-conciliar era is marked by crucial problems and widespread confusion hitherto unknown in recent Church history, but it is also a time of new forward thrusts in important fields. The future stretches ahead both promising and challenging.

POPE PAUL VI

After a very brief conclave, the Cardinals elected good Pope John's successor, Giovanni Battista Montini, who took the name of the great Apostle of the nations, Paul. Cardinal Montini had been the expected choice, since it was well-known that he shared the forward-looking views and hopes of Pope John, and had played a decisive role in the Vatican Council up until then.

A great wave of renewed hope and enthusiasm swept the world at the news of his election. He was loved as a man of great warmth and gentleness, so much like his saintly predecessor, whose close friend he had been. Indeed, it was a known fact that Pope John had had a very high regard for him.

The traveling Pope

"Just as Pope John traveled by train [to the Shrine of Our Lady at Loretto]," people said, "so Pope Paul will travel by plane." And thus it was. As a Cardinal, he had visited North and South America and Africa; now as Pope, he made an unprecedented pilgrimage to the Shrines of the Holy Land, to Nazareth, Bethlehem, Jerusalem — praying with all the ardor of his priestly soul in the Grotto at Bethlehem, in the Garden of Gethsemane, in the Holy Sepulcher....

Unforgettable, indeed, was Pope Paul's meeting with the Eastern Orthodox Patriarch Athenagoras I during this pilgrimage. It was the first such meeting in five hundred years!

On the Mount of Olives, two holy men of God spontaneously embraced one another, in a gesture movingly symbolic of the unity between their Churches so ardently desired by both.

"It is fitting," said the Pope, "that we pilgrims from Rome and Constantinople should meet and join in common prayer." And Athenagoras, in turn, told the Holy Father, "May this meeting be the dawn of a luminous and blessed day, in which future generations will praise and glorify in charity, peace and humility, the one Lord and Savior of the world."

The whole pilgrimage profoundly impressed the world, for it was universally televised. People of every faith held their breath as the Holy Father seemed about to be crushed by the enthusiastic mobs while making his way, in the footsteps of Christ, up the Via Dolorosa to Calvary. Muslims, Jews and Christians, both Orthodox and Catholic—all forgot the things that divided them in their tremendous acclaim of the Pope of Peace, who showed deep emotion at their demonstration of respect.

Wherever he went in the Holy Land, moving scenes occurred. Little Jewish or Arab children waved the papal flag; simple farmers spontaneously came up to offer him coffee; two Muslims waiting to catch a glimpse of him took off their shoes when their hour of prayer struck, faced Mecca, knelt to pray, then went back to stand patiently in line to see the Roman Catholic Pope. It was a truly historic visit, this first airplane trip by a Pope!

"With deeply moved heart," Pope Paul said, back in Rome, "We have returned from Our pilgrimage, and We will carry forever in Our memory the impressive and moving scenes of the holy places which speak with such eloquence of the life of Christ, and of His passion and His love."

The Holy Land
Bombay
The United Nations
Fatima
Ephesus
Bogotá

The ardent spirituality of the Supreme Pontiff won him the world's trust and admiration.

Another historic trip was Pope Paul's visit to the United Nations in New York City, on October 4, 1965, to make a stirring appeal for peace. This was the first visit of a Pope to the United Nations and the first time a Pope had walked on American soil. In a whirlwind fourteen-hour tour, Paul VI conferred with President Johnson on matters of world concern, went to St. Patrick's Cathedral, celebrated Mass at Yankee Stadium — with ninety thousand people participating — and visited the Vatican Pavilion at the New York World's Fair. The great city of New York was completely enthralled by the dramatic event, which by television millions of other Americans, of all faiths, followed the Pope's every step. Through communication satellites, Europe, too, kept its eyes on the dynamic, serenely smiling messenger of peace.

"*Jamais plus la guerre! Jamais plus la guerre!* (No more war! War never again!)" Paul VI implored in his unforgettable speech to representatives of the family of nations.

The United Nations had lost the confidence of many, but the visit of the Pope, whom one journalist described as having "the dignity of the head of a great and ancient Church and the fervor of a simple man seeking peace," powerfully bolstered its prestige. Pope Paul called the UN "the last hope of concord and peace." This Pope of Peace was to continue through various diplomatic channels to try to bring peace to war-torn Vietnam, Palestine and Nigeria.

During his UN speech, which so impressed the world, the Holy Father also spoke on the issue of artificial birth control, which a few years later, was to become the occasion of controversy within the Church. At the UN, Pope Paul appealed for more bread for the tables of the world rather than a favoring of artificial control of births to diminish the number of guests at the banquet of life!

As was to be expected in the new ecumenical era opened by Pope John and Vatican II, Pope Paul had a warm meeting with Protestant, Eastern Orthodox, and Jewish leaders, too. Again, showing another love of his heart, he asked that his motorcade pass through Harlem, one of the poorer sections of New York City. The applause at every stage was deafening and the Holy Father was always joyously responsive, continually blessing the crowds, warming hearts, spreading hope and brotherhood.

Eucharistic Congresses were other occasions for trips by the "traveling Pope." In December, 1964, he went to Bombay, to the great consolation of the comparatively few Catholics of India, and in August, 1968, to Bogotá, Colombia. In 1967, he made two Marian pilgrimages: to Fatima, where Mary had appeared to the three shepherd children in 1917, and to Ephesus, where Mary is believed to have lived with St. John. Everywhere, his obvious grasp of public feeling, his sympathy and understanding, his affectionate, humble ways, his thought-provoking messages, and his prayers for all did much to reawaken supernatural faith and trust, as well as brotherly love, in the hearts of men.

Vatican II —
a Pastoral Council

Never before had there been a council like Vatican II. For one thing, due to modern means of travel, it was the largest in history, there being over two thousand Council Fathers. Secondly, it was mainly a *pastoral* council, which means that its primary concern was not with definition of doctrine but rather with the life of the Church. Pope John had said he hoped that "the Church, Spouse of Christ, may strengthen still more her divine energies and extend her beneficial influence in still greater measure to the minds of men."

The mass media reported in a very "human" fashion the news of the Council Fathers, those whom they termed the "progressives" and those whom they classed as "conservatives." In the customary journalistic way, they looked for the sensational and spoke of "heated debates" or "campaigning for votes" or certain "divisive issues."

The Council Fathers certainly did speak and act in complete freedom, and they certainly had different viewpoints. But, with the Holy Father, they placed their trust in the Holy Spirit, seeking His guidance through fervent prayer. And what a marvelous spectacle of unity they gave to the world despite inevitable differences of opinion!

Vatican II opened on October 11, 1962, and closed on December 8, 1965. There were four sessions in all: from October 11 to December 8, 1962; from September 29 to December 4, 1963; from September 14 to November 21, 1964; and from September 14 to December 8, 1965.

The 16 Documents of Vatican II

In all, the Council issued sixteen documents. The four major *Constitutions* enacted were on *the Church, Divine Revelation, the Liturgy,* and *the Church in the Modern World.*

As someone pointed out, there has never been a more comprehensive study of the Church itself by the official Church than the Constitution produced by Vatican II. THE DOGMATIC CONSTITUTION ON THE CHURCH, therefore, was unique in many ways. It stressed the great mystery of the Church, using biblical figures. In discussing the hierarchical structure of the Church, it explained "collegiality," that is, the authority of the body of bishops and its relations to the primacy of the Pope. It allowed for the restoration of the diaconate as a permanent ministry in the Church. It clarified the position of separated Christians and non-Christians in relation to the Church. It stressed the role of the clergy and the laity in the Church, and the universal call to holiness.

The Church's religious — priests, brothers, and sisters — are portrayed in this document as special witnesses to Christ, and the religious vows as means of more closely following the Lord Jesus and helping others. The final chapter of the Constitution is a treatise on the Mother of God, the Blessed Virgin Mary, who is presented as the perfect model of Christians, the perfect type of the Church.

The DOGMATIC CONSTITUTION ON DIVINE REVELATION discusses the meaning of Revelation, and the handing on of divine Revelation, the nature of tradition and its relation to Scripture, the Old and New Testaments, and Sacred Scripture in the life of the Church. The faithful are urged to nourish themselves abundantly on the "bread of the word of God."

The CONSTITUTION ON THE SACRED LITURGY, which was the very first document promulgated by the Council, gave a new impetus to liturgical renewal, to make the liturgy better understood and more fully participated in by all the People of God. It handled such topics as changes in rites, use of modern languages, concelebration, Communion under both kinds, sacred music, art and furnishings.

The PASTORAL CONSTITUTION ON THE CHURCH IN THE MODERN WORLD excited tremendous interest because of its treatment of so many problems vital to all men: the situation of men in the contemporary world; the Church and man's calling; good and evil in the world; racial discrimination; the arms race; atheism and communism; conscientious objection and military service; marriage and family; relations between the Church and political society; development of culture; underdeveloped nations; peace and the community of nations, etc.

The nine decrees of Vatican II are on the *Pastoral Office of Bishops*, the *Media of Social Communication, Ecumenism, Eastern Catholic Churches*, the *Ministry and Life of Priests, Priestly Training, Adaptation and Renewal of Religious Life*, the *Apostolate of the Laity*, and the *Mission Activity of the Church*.

The three Declarations are on *Christian Education*, the *Relation of the Church to Non-Christian Religions*, and *Religious Freedom*.

Various commissions were set up to interpret and implement the council pronouncements. Especially famous among them were to be the liturgical commission, the commission on the apostolate of the laity, the secretariats for promoting Christian unity, for non-Christian religions and for non-believers.

A particularly notable ecumenical event marked the council's closing period. On December 7, 1965, Paul VI and Patriarch Athenagoras I formally and publicly expressed mutual regret for the excommunication of Michael

Under the guidance of the Holy Spirit,
the Council Fathers labored with love and dedication

Cerularius and two other Eastern churchmen by three papal legates and the counter-excommunication in 1054 of the three papal representatives by the Patriarch Cerularius. They deplored the incidents that followed and finally led to the split between Eastern and Western Christians. This moving expression of regret on the part of contemporary heads of the two Churches was yet another sign of the fast-spreading desire for full Christian unity.

Famous encyclicals of Pope Paul VI

The Development of Peoples

During and after the Council, Pope Paul wrote some masterful encyclicals, one of the most famous being *Populorum Progressio,* on the development of peoples. Written in 1967, it showed the Church's concern for remedying social ills, just as great encyclicals of other modern Popes had done. But *Populorum Progressio* was especially concerned with the new developing nations of the world, such as the African countries which had lately become independent.

Violence and persecution of missionaries, inspired by Communist revolutionaries, had afflicted some areas of Africa during the early days of independence. In the minds of many, the Church had been identified with the Europeans whose domination and influence the native leaders wished to throw off. As a result, in the sixties, some parts of Africa were the scene of violent attacks on the Church and of the martyrdom of a number of dedicated priests and sisters.

One murdered Congolese nun, Sister M. Clementine, is being hailed as the black Maria Goretti, since she died resisting the evil advances of a Communist soldier.

In *Populorum Progressio,* while warning against the evils of violence, the Pope sympathized with the peoples who are striving to escape from hunger, misery, disease and ignorance, who are looking for a wider share in the benefits of civilization. He recognized the damage done by some forms of colonialism, and admitted that the work of missionaries might not be perfect—for nothing human is.

He also stressed, however, the many advantages brought by colonizers and the great good done by missionaries for the native peoples: the schools, hospitals, and orphanages opened by them, in addition to the churches.

"In many a region," he said, "they were the pioneers in material progress as well as in cultural advancement."

The Holy Father sought to awaken the conscience of the world to help the underprivileged peoples. "Private property," he said, "does not constitute for anyone an absolute and unconditional right. No one is justified in keeping for his exclusive use what he does not need, when others lack necessities." He suggested that every man ask himself if he is "prepared to support out of his own pocket works and undertakings organized in favor of the most destitute?...*to leave his country, if necessary and if he is young, in order to assist in this development of the young nations?*"

To achieve world collaboration, Pope Paul made it clear that he considered a world authority necessary. The whole encyclical, like the magnificent ones of his holy Predecessor, good Pope John, strongly appealed to all men to face up to their responsibilities.

On Human Life

Humanae Vitae (on Human Life), was the long-awaited pronouncement on artificial birth control. Issued in the summer of 1968, it stirred up considerable controversy, even more than another encyclical, "Priestly Celibacy." Those Catholics and others who had hoped for a different ruling were dis-

Pope Paul's encyclical showed the Church's
loving concern for the developing nations

appointed that the Vicar of Christ reaffirmed the Church's
ban of artificial methods of birth control.

While stressing the beauty of married love, and also "responsible parenthood," the Holy Father declared: "The Church, calling men back to the observance of the norms of the natural law, as interpreted by their constant doctrine, teaches that each and every marriage act must remain open to the transmission of life."

The encyclical absolutely excludes directly willed and procured abortion, direct sterilization, perpetual or temporary, and "every action which, either in anticipation of the conjugal act, or in its accomplishment, or in the development of its natural consequences, proposes, whether as an end or as a means, to render procreation impossible."

The Holy Father made it clear that he understood well the difficulties of Christian married couples in modern times. But he pointed out the benefits to mankind which come from prayerful, trusting obedience to God's law in these matters. He also made it clear that the Church cannot renounce the teaching of divine law because of human weakness.

A storm of protest met the encyclical, *Humanae Vitae,* which might have been expected in a society wherein sex is glorified and materialistic pleasures are often valued above the riches of the spirit. Many, however, were the heartfelt messages of praise and gratitude which poured into the Holy See. American Methodist Bishop Fred Pierce Corson telegraphed Pope Paul as follows:

"We are grateful for your courage and dedication and your resistance to compromise, for the sake of fashion, between spirit and matter. You are reminding the world of its religious, moral and doctrinal heritage."

An English Catholic couple telegraphed this message: "Peter has spoken; the world does not approve but God approves."

A message from Holland read: "You will receive the gratitude not only of many Dutch parents but also of their children who will realize that they *owe their existence* to the respect of the Church for the natural law."

The journalist-grandson of India's famed Mahatma Gandhi described Pope Paul as a man of courage and added: "By placing conscience above immediate popularity among vocal men, the Pope has set an example for politicians as well as Church officials.

"Moreover, the Pope's views may not be as unpopular as the strident voices opposing them attempt to suggest. A number of people not practicing the disciplines the Pope recommends are nevertheless aware that these are right. They may feel guilty at not practicing them, but many a man would prefer an honest feeling of guilt to the insecurity of a moral desert without standards.

"In an age where blurs constitute art, where a straight line is viewed with suspicion,...Pope Paul has drawn a st aight and precise line. Although intended for the guidance ot Catholics, his encyclical will reward all who read it without prejudice."

In conclusion the article states that men like Paul VI have a simple message: *"There's more to life than popularity and power. There is elegance in simplicity as there is in bravery."*

At a meeting of Catholic physicians in Philadelphia, Dr. G. Papola declared: "Pope Paul was guided by the same God who gave Moses the ten commandments, and it is mandatory on all Catholics, whether laymen or religious, to use their energies in guiding their families, their neighbors, and their communities to follow the laws of God."

The bishops of a number of countries issued statements designed to help their people accept the papal teaching and practice it with faith and trust in God.

Time of crisis

Probably no one expected the post-conciliar period to be an easy one, but it is doubtful whether anyone expected the upheavals, controversy and confusion which became a reality.

It is important to realize, however, that all this cannot be blamed on the Council. Much is the result of certain philosophical currents and secular standards which have gradually influenced many; the "climate of change and renewal" following the Council provided a fertile field for this kind of thinking to make itself heard.

Thoughtful Christians — we and our separated brethren alike — must carefully distinguish between the wonderful forms of renewal called for by the Council and the harmful doctrines or practices which some "self-styled experts" are advocating.

What are the critical areas? One could almost say that few areas indeed were left untouched by confusion and controversy. The Second Vatican Council set the Church out on a magnificent path of renewed fervor and apostolic effectiveness for the benefit of modern man. But, unfortunately, many have interpreted the Council as giving freedom to reject the authority of the Church in favor of private opinion and freedom to revolutionize her doctrines. This was *not* the intention of the Council! In fact, Vatican II aimed to promote greater faithfulness to the Church's mission as defined by Christ: "Go and make disciples of all nations,...*teaching them to observe all that I have commanded you*" (Mt. 28:19-20).

A *relativism in morals* began to be advocated in some quarters. Another term for this same trend is *situation ethics*. Basically, its mistaken principle is that moral decisions are not to be made according to universal moral laws, but rather only to the concrete situation in which a man finds himself in the "here and now." According to this theory, every man would be his own law; the law of God, the obedience we owe Christ and His Church would be ignored.

On September 23, 1967, Pope Paul said: "It is not without considerable sorrow that we have noticed the spread of unacceptable teachings of some who — while playing down the role of the Church's magisterium and depending on false interpretations of the Second Vatican Council—are *recklessly* accommodating Christian moral teaching to tendencies and perverse opinions of our day and age, *as if the law of Christ were supposed to conform itself to this world, and not vice versa."*

Religious instruction, or catechetics, influenced by the pressing racial, economic and peace questions, often turned out to be more a study of sociological factors than of the important supernatural truths of Christian life.

Yet Vatican II's *Declaration on Education* made it clear that catechetical instruction should "enlighten and strengthen the Faith, nourish life according to the spirit of Christ, lead to intelligent and active participation in the liturgical mystery, and give motivation for apostolic activity" (n. 4).

Defections from the priesthood and religious life began to be the cause of great sorrow to the Church. Unfavorable publicity generally accompanied these moves, too. Many of the discontented made public their emotions and complaints, in an immature way, through the press and television, saddening the faithful, their fellow priests and religious, and discouraging prospective vocations. The already critical vocation shortage was thus aggravated. Also, perhaps in a hasty effort to offset the unattractive image portrayed by defections, some religious went to extremes to appear "relevant," "human," "professional," thus watering down the distinctly supernatural witness which the world hopes to find in religious.

The Council documents leave no doubt about what priests and religious are to be! "By the power of the sacrament of Orders, in the image of Christ the eternal high Priest, priests are consecrated to preach the Gospel and shepherd the faithful and to celebrate divine worship..." (Const. on the Church, n. 28). "The religious state clearly manifests that the kingdom of God and its needs, in a very special way, are raised above all earthly considerations." "It is necessary that the members of every community, seeking God solely and before everything else, should join contemplation, by which they fix their minds and hearts on Him, with apostolic love, by which they strive to be associated with the work of Redemption and to spread the kingdom of God" (Const. on the Church, n. 45; Decree on Rel. Life, n. 6).

Liturgical novelty-seekers posed another problem. Some went ahead with unauthorized liturgical experiments, even creating groups known as the *Underground Church*, thus endangering the unity of the Mystical Body for which Christ prayed so ardently.

Open and at times defiant opposition to bishops, particularly on the part of some priests, was another quite new development causing much dismay to the faithful of the postconciliar era. "Why can't they do their objecting quietly and privately?" "Why must they resort to sit-ins, dramatic gestures, and public griping against their bishops?" These became common questions of vast numbers of Catholics.

Had not the Council reemphasized that priests are to be the bishops' cooperators? — "Priests, prudent cooperators with the episcopal order, its aids and instruments, called to serve the people of God, constitute one priesthood with their bishop, although bound by a diversity of duties. Associated with their bishop in a spirit of trust and generosity, they make him present in a certain sense in the individual local congregations.... They are dependent on the bishops in the exercise of their power" (Const. on the Church, n. 28).

"A spirit of corrosive criticism has become the fashion in some sectors of Catholic life," said Pope Paul in September, 1968. "There are, for example, periodicals and newspapers which seem to have no other function than to report unpleasant news relating to ecclesiastical circles. Not infrequently they present such items in a one-sided manner, and possibly slightly altered and dramatized in order to add to their interest and sting. Thus they accustom their readers not to an objective and calm judgment, but on the contrary, to a *negative* point of view, to a systematic distrust, to a preconceived lack of esteem for persons, for institutions, and for activities pertaining to the Church....

"A distinguished Protestant university professor, in a private conversation with Us, referred to this queer mentality as a form of fear — a strange fear of certain Catholics of being regarded as behind the times in the movement of ideas. Thus they are disposed to align themselves with the spirit of the world and to embrace the newest ideas, and those which are most opposed to the customary Catholic tradition. 'Such an attitude, in my opinion,' added the Professor, 'is not in accordance with the spirit of the Gospel.'"

VITAL ACCOMPLISHMENTS
OF THE POST-CONCILIAR CHURCH

On the brighter side, the post-conciliar era is undoubtedly a time of renewed interest in the Church; a time of budding
initiatives designed to bring Christ more fully into men's
lives; a time of increased desire for knowledge of theology
by the laity and for growth in personal holiness; a time of
fuller participation in the sacred liturgy; a time of greater
love for and understanding of our separated brethren.

New life for the liturgy

The progressive *liturgical renewal* brought for the faithful what was perhaps the most striking changes in their lives
as Catholic worshipers. Parts and then almost the whole
Mass began to be said in the vernacular, the language of the
people. The worshiping community participated more and
more actively, in song and spoken word, in the Eucharistic
celebration. Altars were turned so that the celebrant faced the
people, and his actions and prayers were clearly manifest.

Laymen became readers and commentators at Mass. Rites
were simplified, and prayers and readings were varied, although, of course, the essence of the Mass and the adminis-
tration of the sacraments remained the same. The purpose of
the changes was to make the liturgy more meaningful to all.

Despite the dissatisfaction of a minority who did not wish much change, the general response to the liturgical renewal was decidedly enthusiastic. Sacramental life in the Church became more vigorous than ever.

Dialogue within the Church

Another providential development ardently desired by the Second Vatican Council was a more active role within the Church for the laity. The Council of the Laity, right at the Vatican, has prominent lay members from various parts of the world. On the diocesan level, *pastoral councils* were established also to improve communication within the Church.

Pastoral councils are advisory groups of lay men, priests and religious designed to let bishops know what the people of his diocese think and desire for the progress of the Church's work.

A pastoral commission in action

On the parish level, *parish councils* perform the same function. *School boards,* composed mostly of lay men, were rapidly established in thousands of parishes to aid in the operation of the Catholic schools.

Vatican II also envisioned a world *Synod of Bishops* to advise the Pope, and this body met for the first time in September-October, 1967. In the dioceses, *priest senates* were set up to assist bishops in the government of their dioceses. There are also senates or councils of sisters and religious to achieve a closer bond between communities and to coordinate various apostolic activities.

The Church of the post-conciliar period is indeed throbbing with life!

A wonderful age of ecumenism!

In the field of interfaith relations, a marvelous new climate has been created.

Pope Paul continued the tradition of good Pope John in furthering ever more cordial relations with other Christian Churches. Both in the East and at Rome, he met with Patriarch Athenagoras I of the Orthodox Church and with other Orthodox leaders, including Russian and Serbian Patriarchs. He received the Head of the Anglican Church, Archbishop Arthur Michael Ramsey, and began dialogue with the World Council of Churches, which organizes Protestant ecumenical activities.

In the United States, joint Scripture, educational, and publishing projects; frequent meetings and warm dialogue; mutual interest in and sharing of problems related to religion and life; cooperation in promoting peace, justice, and needed legislation — all these have become a reality in a comparatively brief period.

This is true not only on an official level but even on the local community level. It can be said that gatherings of Catholics for solemn occasions are now rarely without separated brethren as guests or participants, and the same is true of the other religious groups. This is truly an ecumenical age!

There is always the danger that individual Catholics may go too far with regard to sharing in liturgical worship with separated brethren, or that some of the faithful may make the mistake of thinking that "after all, religions are pretty much alike and it matters little which one you belong to...." Still, the directives and guidelines on interfaith relations have promoted in general an atmosphere for which all are profoundly grateful to God. The future in this field is a bright one.

Apostolate of the deprived

Urban problems were given special attention in this period. Priests, religious, and a growing number of lay apostles began to dedicate themselves to the spiritual and material uplift of the slum areas afflicted with problems of inadequate housing, low income, racially mixed populations, poor educational and cultural facilities, and discrimination barriers. In the United States, parish churches built for Catholic immigrants who later moved to higher income suburban neighborhoods found themselves unable to cope with the inner city crisis. Team ministry and corporate city-wide financing of new-type apostolates were begun in order to carry out badly needed religious, education and social welfare programs.

"The Church has wed the world!" someone said in viewing the many Church-sponsored projects to combat ignorance, poverty and discrimination.

The Church today on the world scene

In round figures there are about 971,000,000 Christians in the world. Of these, about 596,000,000 are Catholic, 145,000,000 are Eastern Orthodox, and 230,000,000 are Protestant.

Approximately one hundred forty-five million of the Catholics are in Latin America, where there is such a shortage of priests that vast numbers of the people have very little knowledge of doctrine and little opportunity to live a normal Catholic life. The Popes have pleaded for desperately needed missionaries and aid to Latin America, and the response from North America, in particular, has been generous.

Another important observation: in comparison to the approximately forty-seven million Catholics in the United States alone, there are only about forty-six million in all of Asia! And the immense continent of Africa has only about thirty million.

In terms of evangelization, in terms of Christ's mandate, "Go into the *whole world,* and preach the Gospel to *every* creature" — no modern Christian can feel complacent.

Even regarding the lands already won to Christ, our age is no different from past ages in Church history: in other words, there are a thousand pressing needs! The Church lives *in the world,* not apart from it. The spirit of Christ must be made to penetrate every phase of our private, family and social lives: politics, economics, interpersonal and race relations, the arts, education, recreation — everything.

No problem, no need, no injustice, *no person* must be considered outside the sphere of the Church's beneficial influence.

Looking to the future

If there is one thing history has taught us, it is that the Church must reach out to men of *every* age. She must meet them *where they are,* without compromising the heritage of teachings she received from Christ.

No one knows what the future holds for man in the lunar age, in the twenty-first century. But one thing is certain: the Church Christ gave man will always be *young enough, vital enough,* and *loving enough* to serve God and His people as only she can, with the treasures He gave her.

Especially important

▶ TO REFLECT ON:

Love of the Church is not some kind of emotional sensation. It is not a foolish pride that makes a person go around acting superior. It is a humbling thing: who am *I* to have been made a sharer in so rich an experience? It is a realistic appreciation of the marvelous community of love that is the Church, a community which is also a sign of Christ's presence among us, a community in which we are fed with the bread of Christ's word and the Bread of His body. Love of the Church, loyalty to her, is the same as love and loyalty to Christ.

▶ TO STRIVE FOR:

Never before have men sought unity as they seek it today. *Strive to build bridges* — bridges between people who are now strangers because of differing beliefs or races or neighborhoods. To be a bridge-builder, you will have to be a true lover of your God, your Church (which by her very name is catholic, "universal"), and your brothers in God. This will nearly always mean sacrificing yourself time and time again, while never sacrificing your Faith.

▶ TO TALK TO GOD ABOUT:

O Lord, make us, your disciples and followers, submit ourselves free and docile to the mystery of the unity which is your Church, living in your truth and love. O Lord, may our love for all our brothers in Christ become more ardent and active for an ever more intense collaboration with them in the building of the kingdom of God. O Lord, make us understand better how to unite our efforts with all men of good will, to realize fully the good of humanity in truth, liberty, justice and love. We thus pray to you, O Christ, who with the Father and the Holy Spirit, lives and reigns, God, forever and ever. Amen.

POPE PAUL VI

Two thousand years is a long time. No other institution on the face of the earth ever lasted that long. But just "to last" is not as important as "to grow." And the Church — human-divine marvel that she is — grows, renews herself, and weathers every storm, ever beginning again to heal the wounds in man's spirit and body, century after century.

Imperial Rome is but a memory. The feudal castles have crumbled. The thrones of yesteryear are no more. But the Church that saw all that glory come and go will never fail, as her Divine Founder promised. With the wisdom of the sage and the daring of the astronaut, she lifts her face to the future — humble, confident, eager to serve.

STUDY QUESTIONS

1   The First Brothers in Christ

1. How would you describe Christ's attitude toward people?
2. What special responsibilities, promises and powers did Jesus give His apostles?
3. What is Jesus Christ's place in history?
4. What significant role did Abraham have in pre-Christian history?
5. What was Moses' role?
6. What is meant by saying that in Jesus Christ God established a New Covenant with men?
7. What books of the Bible show us the first years of the Church and the conduct of the first Christians?
8. What especially characterized the early Christians?
9. What event was instrumental in spreading the Faith outside Jerusalem?
10. How did God show St. Peter, the head of the Church, that he was to accept for Baptism not only Jews but also any sincere person of any race or nationality?
11. How did St. Paul come to realize that Christ and His followers *are one* — so that to love Christ is to love the brethren?

2   Conquest through Suffering

1. In what way was the highly developed Roman state a help in spreading the Faith? In what way was this empire an obstacle?
2. What were the effects of the preaching of the Gospel in pagan Rome?
3. Why did the emperors persecute the Christians?
4. How did the greater number of Christians react to the persecutions?
5. What is the importance of Constantine in Christian history?
6. Why are heresies as great a danger as persecution?
7. What was the Arian heresy?
8. Who are some of the Fathers of the Church, and what did they do to deserve the high honor paid them?
9. What effect has St. Augustine had on history?
10. How did the Church meet the challenge of the barbarian invasions?
11. Why can it be said that the monks rebuilt Europe?
12. Who is the outstanding Pope of this period and what were some of his accomplishments?

3   Light and Darkness

1. Why were Popes often obliged to act as temporal rulers and defenders of the people against attacks?
2. What is meant by the Patrimony of Peter?
3. What was the Iconoclast heresy?
4. Why is Charlemagne so famous in Church history?
5. What was meant by "Holy Roman Empire"?
6. State the two main teachings of Islam.
7. What was the extent of the Mohammedan conquests?
8. What groups were invaders in the Dark Ages?
9. Who was mainly responsible for the eleventh century reform?
10. How did the abbey of Cluny help restore fervor among religious?
11. What is meant by "lay investiture"?
12. What was the purpose of the Crusades? Who inspired them?
13. Were the Crusades successful as a whole?
14. How did the split between Christians of the West and East come about?

4   A Vibrant, Violent Age

1. What ancient error did the Cathari or Albigensians revive?
2. What social evils did this sect bring?
3. How was it finally checked?
4. What was the Inquisition? Why did the Popes protest against this institution as it was conducted in some regions?
5. What was the nature of the conflict between Pope Boniface VIII and King Philip IV?
6. Why was the papal residence at Avignon called the Babylonian captivity?
7. What do we mean by the "great Western schism"?
8. Explain the "conciliar problem."
9. How did the religious life develop?
10. What is the difference between monks and friars?
11. In what way was St. Francis of Assisi the answer to the Church's needs in his day?
12. What are some of the glories of medieval culture?
13. What great developments took place in learning in the late Middle Ages?
14. What was the lasting achievement of St. Thomas Aquinas.

5   Break-Up

1. What was the extent of Christianity in Europe at the beginning of the fifteenth century?
2. What is meant by the "Renaissance"?
3. Who were some of the great Italian Renaissance artists?
4. What were some of the harmful effects of the Renaissance?

5. What was the deplorable state of the papacy which prevented the much-needed reform?

6. Who was Savonarola?

7. What is meant by the national spirit?

8. What monarchs were called the "Catholic Sovereigns"? What did they accomplish?

9. Who were Wycliffe and Hus?

10. How would you summarize the causes leading up to the break from the Church?

11. What was Martin Luther's great personal problem? How did he solve it?

12. If Luther at first did not intend to break with the Church, how did the break come about?

13. What were some of Luther's main teachings?

14. Who was Zwingli? What did Luther think of these newer doctrines?

15. In what ways did John Calvin differ from Luther?

16. What did Calvin mean by predestination?

17. Why can we say that Calvinism was a more organized religion than Lutheranism?

18. Who was John Knox?

19. How was the Church affected by the drama involving King Henry VIII, Catherine of Aragon, and Anne Boleyn?

20. What title and position did Henry assume?

21. Who were Thomas More and John Fisher?

22. What happened to Catholicism in England during the reigns of Edward VI, Mary, and Elizabeth?

6   Renewal Within and a Hardening of the Walls

1. What were the achievements of the Council of Trent?

2. How did Ignatius Loyola fulfill his motto: "For the greater glory of God"?

3. What events especially set off a new missionary effort?

4. How was the faith planted in North and South America?

5. Who is the great missionary to the Orient?

6. What country of the Far East was the site of Christian persecutions?

7. What methods did Father Ricci use to present Christianity to the Chinese?

8. What is the importance of the battles of Lepanto and Vienna?

9. How did Orthodox Christianity develop in Russia?

10. Why did Protestants and Catholics grow further and further apart?

11. What was the Edict of Nantes?

12. Would you say that "Most Christian King" was a proper title for Louis XIV?

13. What was Jansenism?

14. What was Quietism?

15. Which European countries remained predominantly Catholic? Which were predominantly Protestant?

16. What was St. Vincent de Paul's special contribution to the Church's apostolate?

7   A Time of Revolt

1. What is rationalism?

2. What harmful effect did the separation of faith and reason have?

3. Explain the confusion surrounding the "Galileo affair."

4. Who was Voltaire?

5. What is meant by the term, "Protestant revivalism"?

6. Why did new sects constantly appear within Protestantism?

7. Describe the religious origins of the United States.

8. Why did John Carroll and other Catholic Americans rejoice at the proclamation of the Constitution?

9. Who was Elizabeth Seton?

10. How did the inhuman slave trade affect the religious history of the Negro people?

11. Why is the French Revolution a sorrowful chapter in the history of the Church?

12. What was Napoleon's religious policy?

13. What temporal loss did the Church suffer during the reign of Pope Pius IX?

14. What dogma did the First Vatican Council define?

15. Why can it be said that the Catholic Church showed "new vigor" at the close of the Nineteenth Century?

8   The Popes and the World

1. What problem did the Church under Pope Leo XIII face in Germany?

2. Who was Félicité de La Mennais?

3. Who were some of the early champions of liberty and social progress for the common people, for the workers?

4. Why is *Rerum Novarum* such an important document?

5. What is meant by the Oxford Movement?

6. What three major problems faced the Church in the United States?

7. What is meant by *trusteeism*?

8. In what ways did anti-Catholic sentiment show itself in the United States?

9. Why was Cardinal Gibbons' action concerning the Knights of Labor so important?

10. Why is Pope St. Pius X known as the "Pope of the Eucharist"?

11. What did Pius X do for church music and catechetics?

12. What was the Modernist heresy?

13. What role did the Vatican play during the First World War?

14. What was Pius XI's policy regarding the priesthood in mission lands?

15. What developments took place in religious orders?

16. Describe the Mexican persecution.

17. What was the Lateran Treaty and how did it change the temporal situation of the Holy See?

18. How did the Fascist and Nazi dictatorships come into conflict with the Church under Pope Pius XI?

19. What three major documents did Pius XI issue against three totalitarian systems?

20. Which one of these systems is still persecuting the Church?

9   Defenders of Peace and Good Will

1. What great tragedy struck at the very beginning of Pope Pius XII's reign?

2. What efforts did Pius XII make to end the war and to bring relief to war victims?

3. In particular, what did the Holy Father do for the Jews?

4. What is meant by the term "Church of Silence"?

5. What is the aim of international Communism, and why does it systematically persecute the Church?

6. What Marian dogma did Pope Pius XII define?

7. What famous encyclical letter did he write on the nature of the Church?

8. What new form of consecrated life did he approve?

9. In what way was Pope John XXIII's background and personality similar to that of Pope Pius X?

10. What does Pope John's diary reveal about his spiritual life?

11. When did John XXIII announce the Second Vatican Council and what were some of its objectives?

12. What was the subject of the famous encyclical, *Mater et Magistra?*

13. What was the subject of Pope John's last encyclical?

10   The Council and After

1. Why was there general rejoicing at the election of Cardinal Montini as Pope John's successor?

2. Why did Pope Paul's trip to the Holy Land win world attention?

3. What other trips by the Holy Father followed upon that first one?

4. What historic appeal did Paul VI make at the United Nations in New York City in 1965?

5. Why can it be said that there had never been an ecumenical council like the Second Vatican Council?

6. Name the sixteen documents of Vatican II.

7. Summarize the four major documents.

8. What three Vatican secretariats set up after the Council relate to those outside the Catholic Church?

9. Name and summarize two famous encyclicals of Pope Paul VI.

10. What are some of the causes of confusion and controversy in the Church today?

11. What is meant by "situation ethics"?

12. Would you say that many doctrinal and moral errors being spread result from a desire to make Christ's teachings conform to the world?

13. What did Pope Paul mean by saying that "a spirit of corrosive criticism has become the fashion in some sectors of Catholic life"?

14. What benefits has the liturgical renewal brought?

15. What are pastoral councils?

16. What is the Synod of Bishops?

17. Summarize the ecumenical developments of the postconciliar period.

18. In what way are the problems of the big cities being faced by Christians in our day?

19. Why does Latin America have a special need for missionaries?

20. What does the future hold for the Church?

INDEX

"Te Deum" 134
Tekakwitha, Kateri 130
telescope 157
television 196, 237
temperament 127
ten commandments 22, 235
Teresa of Avila, St. 125, 137, 151, 178
"Testem Benevolentiae" 189
Thaddeus, St. Jude 24
Theatines 125
theft 22, 113
Theodolinda, Queen, St. 47
Theodosius 34
theologians 106, 123, 136, 140
theology 44, 74, 86, 87, 89ff., 97, 104, 136, 192
Therese of Lisieux, St. 31, 178
Thirty Years War 128
Thomas Aquinas, St. 90, *91*, 106, 183
Thomas a Becket, St. 78f., 79, 83, 92
Thomas More, St. 114f., *114*
Toniolo 182
totalitarian states 199ff.
"tracts" 184
tradition 229
traditions, Protestant 136
Trajan 38
transubstantiation
  denial of doctrine of 104
treason 80, 81
treaties 138
Trent, Council of 123f., 134, 139, 142, 179
Trinity, the 20
"trusteeism" 186
truth 29, 92, 155, 184
  supernatural 237
Turkish Empire 135
Turks 64, 97, 134, 136
Twelve Apostles 25

U

underdeveloped nations 217, 230, 232f.
"Underground Church" 237
underprivileged peoples 233
union(s)
  labor 182, 186
Unitarians 160
United Nations 218, 227
United States 129, 130, 162ff., 170, 185, 187ff., 190, 207, 209, 227, 241
unity 48, 108, 118, 178, 179, 186, 243
  among Christians 69
  rupture in 111
universality of the Church 30, 117; see also *Church*
universality of God's plan 21f.
universe, creation of 21

universities 74, 90, 92, 97, 99, 156
University of Oxford 184
University of Paris 92
Urban II, Pope 64f.
Urban VI, Pope 81ff.
urban problems 242
Ursulines 125
"Utopia" 114

V

Valerian 38
Vandals 45
Vatican, the 190, 192, 194
  archives of 183
Vatican City 198f., 207f., 214
Vatican radio 196, 199
Vatican Secretariat for Non-Christians 18ff.
Vatican I 154, 172
Vatican II 173; see also *ecumenical councils*
  Documents of 229ff.
  teaching of 222
vernacular 239
Vicar of Jesus Christ 177
  see also *Popes*
Vienna 135
Vietnam 209, 227
Vikings 60
Vincent de Paul, St. 125, 126, 141, 148, 149, *149*, 150, 165, 196
  Conferences of 182
violence 136, 140, 148
Virginia 161
virgins 84
visible head of the Church 30
Visigoths 45, 48
visions 27, 174
Visitation Nuns 125
Vitus, St. 40
vocations 121, 237
Voltaire, Francois-Marie 155, 157f.
von Bismark, Count 180
von Bora, Katherine 107
von Groot, Hugo 148
Von Ketteler, Bishop 182
vows 107; see also *poverty, chastity and obedience*

W

Waldensians 146
war(s) 64ff., 102, 138, 143, 177, 193, 194
Wartburg, Germany 127
Washington, George 164˙
Watts 156
wealthy, the 97, 100, 102, 110
Wesley, Charles 159
Wesley, John 158f.

Daughters of St. Paul

In Massachusetts
50 St. Paul's Avenue, *Boston*, Mass. 02130
172 Tremont Street, *Boston*, Mass. 02111
In New York
78 Fort Place, *Staten Island*, N.Y. 10301
625 East 187th Street, *Bronx*, N.Y. 10458
525 Main Street, *Buffalo*, N.Y. 14203
In Connecticut
202 Fairfield Avenue, *Bridgeport*, Conn. 06603
In Ohio
2105 Ontario St. (at Prospect Ave.), *Cleveland*, Ohio 44115
In Pennsylvania
1127 South Broad Street, *Philadelphia*, Pa. 19147
In Florida
2700 Biscayne Blvd., *Miami*, Florida 33137
In Louisiana
4403 Veterans Memorial Blvd., Metairie, *New Orleans*, La. 70002
86 Bolton Avenue, *Alexandria*, La. 71301
In Texas
114 East Main Plaza, *San Antonio*, Texas 78205
In California
1570 Fifth Avenue, *San Diego*, Calif. 92101
278 17th Street, *Oakland*, Calif. 94612
46 Geary Street, *San Francisco*, Calif. 94108
In Canada
3022 Dufferin Street, *Toronto* 395, Ontario, Canada
In England
57, Kensington Church Street, *London* W. 8, England
In Australia
58, Abbotsford Rd., Homebush, N.S.W., *Sydney* 2140, Australia
In Philippine Islands
2650, F.B. Harrison, P.O. Box 3576, *Pasay City*, Manila,
Philippine Islands
In India
143, Waterfield Road, Bandra, *Bombay*, 50-AS, India
In Africa
35, Jones Street, P.O. Box 3243, *Lagos*, Nigeria